WALK

A

LITTLE

FARTHER

WITH

ME

BY

JOHNNIE CLARK

Scripture quotations taken from the New American Standard Bible® (NASB),
Copyright © 1960, 1962, 1963, 1968, 1971, 1972, 1973, 1975, 1977, 1995 by The Lockman Foundation.
Used by permission. www.Lockman.org

First Edition 2019
ISBN: 978-1075309441

www.johnnieclark.com

My thanks, love, and praise to Jesus Christ for the miracle of a lifetime and a million other gifts.

Much love and countless thanks to Nancy, Shawn, Bonnie and Gunner: I'd be lost without you.

My love and thanks to these wonderful friends for all of your help in getting this book out.

To Tori McGee, my Girl Friday: how did I ever write books without you?

To Laura, Luke, Rick, and Robb for their belief, encouragement, and editing.

To Philski, Duffy, and Many Numbers.

Thank you, Lord, for putting these people in my life.

WALK A LITTLE FARTHER WITH ME

I wrote a best seller titled *Guns Up!,* and I wrote it in first person because I didn't know how to write any other way. All of my other books are third person. Like *Guns Up!,* this story can't be written any other way but in first person. And, no matter how I write it—first person or third person—that person is going to sound like they've been drinking way too much Tullamore Dew. But the miracle I'm about to go public with is the absolute truth, and I'll be happy to swear it on anyone's Bible or tell it in anyone's church.

That being said, I won't blame anyone for thinking this guy's still suffering from combat fatigue. And they'd be partially on target; I was diagnosed with severe combat fatigue when I came home from Nam. To please the PC police, it's now called PTSD, but the term combat fatigue is more appropriate in my case.

The events in this story did not happen because of combat fatigue, but that did play a role in how God put me on a mountain called Graybeard in the middle of North Carolina.

I had never heard of Graybeard Mountain in my life. But God spoke to me on that mountain. It was as simple and phenomenal as that. How He got my attention and what He did makes this the most difficult and most important book I've ever attempted.

I've written several war books about my beloved Marine Corps, which is how I met a remarkable hero named Mitchell Paige. This book will have a few war stories from two different wars because God used war and machine guns to put Mitch and me together.

Sgt. Mitchell Paige, Medal of Honor, Guadalcanal. Sgt. Mitchell Paige is the man that Hasbro Toys made the G.I. Joe doll in honor of. We were both Marine machine gunners, and how God connected us and this miracle will hopefully move and inspire you. Frankly I hope it blows your mind the way it has mine.

1

WEST VIRGINIA

I want to introduce myself so you know exactly who this less-than-saintly character is who's writing about miracles. So before we go to that mountain in North Carolina, I want to take you to the mountains I came from in West—by God—Virginia. I grew up in poverty. When I was a baby, we lived in a cabin that had newspaper on the walls to stop the wind and bugs from coming in, or so I was told by my Grandpa. When I was five, we lived in a one-car garage in South Charleston across the alley from my Grandma and Grandpa Clark. They were pretty rough people.

My Grandpa Clark once shot a guy with a shotgun. One version of the story that I was told was that a jealous nut case had been pounding on their door threatening to kill my aunt. I've also heard other versions of the story, but the point is, he shot the guy. Some of that guy's blood was on the wall of my garage house. Adults tried to tell me it was red paint, but even as a five-year-old, I knew better.

My uncles were known as the Clark brothers. There was one gentle uncle in the group of four, Uncle Jimmy. He was my babysitter sometimes, and a more tender man didn't exist. But even gentle Jimmy once picked up a full-grown man and threw him through the big window of the Victory Theater.

According to my uncles, my dad was the toughest fighter of the clan and was so admired for his fighting skill that the brothers once started a barroom brawl and then all stepped back just to watch him in action. Another time Billy and Bobby Clark, who are two very tough men, jumped Dad as a prank one night. Uncle Jack told me that Dad beat the crap out of his two very tough brothers.

My Great-Grandmother Clark was known as Little Grandma. She was only about four feet five, while Great-Grandpa Clark was six feet six. They made a very funny couple. Little Grandma was the sweetest person I've ever known. She was a full-blooded Native American, or so I was told, and she sure looked like an "Indian." I was told that Little Grandma and many others from her tribe had changed their last name to Knuckles to fit in better. Maybe it's just family legend.

On my mom's side of the family were the McClellans. They were real country folk, not that the Clarks weren't very country also. But the McClellans lived up the holler from the McCoys and down the holler from the Hatfields in Lincoln County. They were tough farmers and coal miners. Grandpa McClellan carved a farm out of 160 acres of mountains. Even as a little boy, I was amazed that my Grandpa and my mom's twelve brothers and sisters had plowed the sides of hills into a farm. I don't think Americans have the grit to work that hard now.

When times were hard, some of the McClellan boys and Grandpa had to work in the coal mines. Working the mines was not for sissies. Uncle Roy McClellan was my Dad's best friend and my Mom's favorite brother. He died when the mine he was working caved in. Many years later in 1976, Grandpa McClellan died of black lung disease. Grandpa McClellan's funeral gave me a few memories that will always stay with me, but one specific incident was right out of a movie scene.

I was standing outside the old country church waiting to go inside for the funeral with two of my uncles, Jack and Bobby Clark. Four crusty looking older gentlemen rode up to the church on big brown horses that glistened with sweat from a long ride. Each man had a ZZ Top type beard, long and pointed. These guys looked as if they'd just come from a Civil War movie set. Three of the men wore gray, wide-brimmed hats that had seen newer days and the fourth wore a brown one. I don't remember the colors of their clothes but they wore three-piece suits that appeared to be from a bygone era, and plain black boots that were worn and comfortable looking.

Each old man had a long-barreled Colt .45 pistol on his hip, and at least two of them actually had CSA (Confederate States of America) belt buckles. I'm a bit of history buff and these buckles sure looked like the real thing. I was told by an old man standing nearby that it was a great honor to my Grandpa that they had come, because these men had not been seen in years and rarely came out of the mountains.

* * * * *

When I was five years old, my dad was in a terrible car crash and a State Trooper came to our garage house to tell my mom that he wasn't expected to live. He had been pronounced dead at the scene, but someone massaged his heart and revived him. I remember that night vividly. It was snowing, and the State Trooper returned later that same night to give me a jack-in-the-box toy that played "Silent Night." Funny how those moments stay with you.

My dad survived but was blind and in a full body cast for a year and lost his memory for longer than that. He had no clue who any of us were. It was like living with a mummy. I remember bringing my five and six year old friends in to see him lying on a little bed behind a curtain that was his bedroom. It was always dark, since there were no windows, but it didn't matter because Dad was blind. He really did look like "The Mummy," so it spooked my friends. My mom was incredible in the way she took care of him. We're talking bed pans and urinals and trying to keep him clean in a full body cast for a year. I don't know how she did it.

Watching dad suffer like that was hard, and watching my mom trying to take care of us was just as bad. We had no money. She made seventy dollars each month ironing clothes for neighbors. I know this is probably starting to sound like the guy who walked uphill in both directions to school, but this is just the way things happened. And in spite of the poverty, I was a very happy kid.

I had brothers and sisters, but poverty kept us apart. My mom, Opal, had two children named Jimmy and Judy from her first marriage to Howard Soper. Howard was killed in the Battle of the Bulge in 1945. Mom gave Jimmy and Judy to their dad's grandparents in Wilmore, Kentucky. They raised Howard because his parents were dead. It was supposed to be temporary, just until she was able to take care of them. But she remarried and had more children, and there never was enough money to bring her older kids home. The Sopers were wonderful Christian people, and Grandpa

Soper had actually been a Circuit Rider for the Methodist Church many years before.

Mom met my dad after the war. They married and had my sister, Evelyn. Dad lost his job right after she was born, and Evelyn was given to Mom's parents, the McClellans, to keep and feed until they got on their feet. That never happened. So Evelyn grew up on the McClellan farm. Sis was in the first class to graduate Hatfields and McCoys together. That feud was the most famous feud in American history, and we feel sort of a part of it because, years later, my sister married Kirby McCoy.

The Sopers and the McClellans were wonderful people and did a fine job raising Mom's kids. But Mom regretted not being able to raise us together for the rest of her life. I was the baby and Opal was holding on to her last child at any cost. On those occasions we were together it was joyful, I love Jimmy and Judy and Evelyn very much. But the joy was quickly followed by deep sadness at being separated. I always felt a sense of guilt about being the only kid Mom kept. Poverty or not, I got to stay with our Mom and they didn't.

* * * * *

Dad lived for almost seven years after the horrific car crash. He got his memory back after a year and a half but was blind and crippled until he died.

My father came to the Lord during those seven years. I was with him when Grandpa Clark and a preacher helped him into a cold mountain river to baptize him. In spite of his awful condition, Dad became a powerful Christian and a witness to everyone. I believe it took that terrible car wreck to bring Dad to the Lord, and during those years he led many others to Christ including me. Of course, it is easy to see God's hand in all of this in hindsight, but it wasn't so easy when we were going through it.

* * * * *

We moved to a Quonset hut when I was eight. It had been a military hut that a very sweet elderly lady named Miss Alice White rented out. Our situation was pretty obvious, and Miss White lowered our rent enough for us to be able to afford it.

As a little kid, I was sort of proud that I lived in the only round house on Brown Street. I honestly never thought about how poor we were until one awful day in the fifth grade. That day is one of those indelible memories that we all have. It is a memory so embarrassing that sixty years hasn't faded it away. It all started during the Brown Street war.

I was the leader of a gang of kids known as the Brown Street gang. It wasn't a gang in the vicious sense of the word. We built tree houses and clubhouses out of scraps of wood and forts out of snow in the winter. We were building maniacs. Sometimes we had rock wars with the Blackwell Street gang. Looking at it now, it was downright dangerous at times. Of course, we always took care to be safe during these wars. We wore old WWII army leggings, and those who had them wore gas masks and coal miner helmets.

One day, the Blackwell Street gang rode by on their bikes and strafed our fort with machine guns. Now, a machine gun was a hand full of pebbles in a handkerchief. You held one corner of the handkerchief between forefinger and thumb and held the other three corners in your fist. If a kid on a bike was good at it, he could spray an area twenty feet wide with rocks.

It was a great weapon, which I had invented. The enemy had now stolen my design and turned it against us. We had an emergency meeting of our generals. It was obvious that our engineers needed to come up with the ultimate weapon to combat the buzz bombers . . . that's enemy bicycles in adult lingo.

We needed artillery! My best friend was a chubby blond-haired kid named Eddie Pritt. I loved Eddie, and we had cut fingers to become blood brothers. Eddie and I and the Dodrill brothers went to work on our design. We built a giant slingshot. It was a labor of love and war. Within a couple of days we had fashioned two-by-fours and an old automobile tire's inner-tube into a sophisticated piece of long range artillery.

Our clubhouse was in an empty lot beside my round house. We knew that spies from Blackwell Street had seen us digging the hole to mount the giant slingshot, but they had not seen the actual weapon. We had constructed it in a secret location. Finally, the time came to carry it out and mount it for test firing. It was apparent immediately that it would take more muscle than most of us had to fire the weapon. Eddie was chubby and stout as a horse and was the obvious choice. It would take special ammunition, and we'd collected a stack of smooth round rocks from a creek on Springhill Mountain.

Test firing was a total success, but even Eddie was having a tough time pulling that inner-tube back, so I assigned Corporal Ronnie Dodrill to help him. As commanding general, I naturally would give the final commands to ready, aim, and fire.

Our spy was a girl named Debbie Crook, who could climb trees almost as well as a boy. She was in a tall maple tree at the end of the street with a red towel to signal when the buzz bombers approached. That would give us time to load the artillery piece. Soon, the red towel was waving from the tree top, and our men in the trench in front of the clubhouse readied their ammo.

I raised my arm like the starter of a race and yelled, "Artillery Ready!"

"Aim!"

The enemy planes roared past as fast as they could pedal. Our clubhouse sounded like it was being pelted by a hail storm. I lowered my arm and screamed.

"Fire!"

Our big round river rock ripped into the spokes of an enemy buzz bomber, and he went down in a heap of pedals and handle bars! We cheered as the enemy circled for another pass.

"Reload!"

In the heat of battle, I had not noticed that Corporal Dodrill was down and wounded with a round just under his coal miner's helmet and above the left eye. I think he was bleeding and crying, but there was no time for the wounded as I rushed to help Eddie reload. Like any new weapon that has to be rushed into combat, our giant slingshot had to be built with the materials at hand. We fully expected some kinks would have to be worked out. However, as general, I had not anticipated a catastrophic failure.

Eddie and I loaded the next round and were waiting for the perfect moment to open fire. As the enemy raced closer, we pulled with all our strength and braced ourselves. It took courage to stand our ground while enemy bullets pelted all around us, but we did. I think that's when I first heard that awful creaking sound and knew that using that 2x4 with the yellow paint had been a bad idea. The crack was deafening as it fully gave way.

To this day, I'm not sure if that's when it happened or not. The fog of war can be confusing. But in reviewing after action reports, I determined that was when I ripped the seat of my pants. That doesn't seem like a big deal. But the ripple effect it had on me became a lifelong memory.

I only had three pairs of pants. I had one pair of nice pants and one nice shirt that could be worn only for church on Sunday. I had one pair of pants that could be worn only to school. And I had one pair of play pants. None of these pants were new, but they were always clean. In the rush and heat of preparation for battle, I had stupidly worn my school pants to war. Mom had no choice but to allow me to wear my church clothes to school that following Monday.

My fifth grade teacher had broken a couple of rulers over my head during the year. I smiled all the time. I'm sure you knew goofy kids who smiled all the time. Well, I was one of those. I even smiled when I was being yelled at. This teacher thought I was making fun of her, so she would crack me on the head. I'm sure I deserved it for other reasons she didn't know about, but I don't think I should have been cracked for smiling.

After most of the year went by, she finally realized that I wasn't being disrespectful and wrote my mom a letter apologizing. She explained that she basically had thought I was a wise guy but now understood that I was just a happy kid. I think that was why she made such a big deal about it when I walked into the classroom a little late and looking a lot nicer than usual.

"My, my look at you, Johnnie! You look so nice today," she said with a big smile. Then she faced the entire class. "Class, doesn't Johnnie look nice today?" So for the rest of that day other kids would come up to me and say something nice about the way I was dressed.

That was it. That was the day I realized that we were poor. From that moment on I started noticing all the stuff I had never given a thought to because I was too busy being happy. When I went home from school that day, my round house wasn't as neat as it had been. When mom fixed supper that night, I noticed that some of our food came out of military green WWII government cans. Up to that day, I actually thought Spam was sort of the same thing as steak since I'd never tasted steak. And the list grew, especially as I started liking girls. It was not easy to impress girls on a bike put together from parts of old bikes that were all different colors.

When I was ten years old, I overheard my dad praying for the Lord to take him home. Of course he thought he was alone when he prayed, but I would often sit quietly and listen to my dad pray. He talked to God like you would talk to a friend. Dad thought he was a terrible burden on everyone, especially since he could do nothing to earn income for the family. He asked the Lord to take him home to ease everyone's burden.

Not long after that prayer, my dad died. I was ten years old. The adults were worried about me because I didn't cry at the funeral. A few days later, I was playing with a bunch of friends when one kid said, "You must have not loved your dad 'cuz you don't even care that he died." I went into a rage and beat the tar out of that kid. I kept beating him until adults pulled me off of him, and then I cried for a long time.

I never forgot about my dad's prayer to go home, uttered just days before his death. It left me with a fearful respect for the power of prayer.

2

UNITED STATES MARINES

Mom and I moved to St. Petersburg, Florida, after Dad died. I was eleven. She wanted to go to the sunshine and away from a lot of painful memories. When I was fourteen, Mom married a tough old ex-Navy man named Paul Lampe. He was a good man and had been a golden gloves boxer from Hell's Kitchen in New York.

St. Petersburg was wonderful in the early sixties. My days at St. Pete High School were some of the happiest of my life. It was like going to a small college, nothing like most high schools today. I wish my children could have experienced a high school like mine. I majored in football, baseball, and cheerleaders. It was a time when the radio played the Beach Boys and The Beatles, and America was still mostly a Christian nation.

We were at war when I graduated in 1967. My mom didn't know it, but I had already joined the Marine Corps before graduation on a delayed entry program. At seventeen my stepdad, Paul, had to sign for me. Breaking that news to my mom wasn't easy. She got pretty upset and begged me to go into any other service but the Marines. I still remember her screaming at me, "Marines are the first ones in and the first ones to die!"

It got pretty emotional, and it took some fast talking to calm her down. With tears in her eyes, she finally admitted that she'd always known I would go into the Marine Corps some-day.

"You've been telling me that since you were five years old," she said as she started crying.

Paul and I did even more fast talking to calm her down again. She was glad to hear that three of my buddies were joining up with me, or so we thought. At the last moment, all three pulled out, and that bus drive to the induction center in Jacksonville sure felt lonely.

I was seventeen, extremely naïve, and far from the sharpest tack in the box, but I was a very patriotic and dedicated kid. The previous fall, I'd played my last two games of high school football on a broken ankle that had been taped together. The doctor later told me I could have been crippled for life if the bones had come apart. We won the city and county championship, though.

Like I said, I was not the sharpest tack in the box.

* * * * *

I was afraid that the war would be over before I got there. It was 1968 when we landed in Da Nang, and the Tet Offensive was in full swing. My best pal in the Corps and bunkie at Parris Island was a Chinese American Marine named PFC Richard Chan. We stayed together for my entire time in the Corps. Chan was older and a college grad who planned to become an open-heart surgeon after the war. He had his pre-med degree, a minor in ministry, and was a genius. You're probably asking why a genius was a PFC Machine Gunner in the Marines. We all wondered that same thing. Why wasn't he an officer or a Navy doctor?

Chan had been smuggled out of Red China as a baby. His father was a doctor, and they escaped Communism. Chan wanted to pay

America back for taking his family in. He knew that the Marines were America's best and that they would be meeting the Communists face to face, so he wanted to be a Marine. How can you not love a guy like that?

PFC RICHARD CHAN

The battle for Hue City had covered the front pages of every newspaper back home. On TV, the house-to-house fighting looked like World War II films. The famous 5th Marine Regiment was retaking Hue City, and casualties were heavy, so we were excited but not surprised when the big rubber stamp came down on our orders in Da Nang and a crusty Sergeant shouted, "Fifth Marines!"

Twenty minutes later we were herded into a waiting C-130 for a short flight north to a place called Phu Bai. The plane ride would have been more comfortable with seats or windows and no rifles sticking in our ribs. I wasn't scared because, as an eighteen-year-old Marine, I was going to live forever, but there sure was a lot sweat coming out of my pores.

Phu Bai was the base camp for the Fifth Marines. It didn't look like a dangerous place. One part even looked fairly civilized, with groups of tin-roofed houses made of wood and screens. Sandbag bunkers dotted the camp, and everything was colored beige over green from the dust of tanks, trucks, and jeeps rolling through the dirt streets. I soon found out that the civilized part of Phu Bai belonged to the Army. The Marine area was all dust-covered WWII-era tents.

The Second Platoon tent consisted of two rows of cots. At the end of one row, dwarfing the small cot he slept on, rested a giant redheaded man. His arms looked as big as my thighs, and he must have had on size fifteen jungle boots. His boots were so crusty that they looked like moccasins, and his utilities were bleached beige from the sun and jungle rain. He had a big red moustache and was probably the most handsome redheaded man I'd ever seen. He looked like the Marlboro man in the cigarette commercials.

CPL. RICHARD WEAVER

Chan led the way as we walked to the end of the tent and sat on the cot beside him. I wasn't sure what he might think, since the rest of the tent was empty. It was sort of like standing in a large bathroom with a dozen urinals and having some clown take the one right next to you. But I didn't care because I had a million questions about this adventure we just walked into called Vietnam, and this giant Viking was going to answer some scuttlebutt. Chan must have felt the same way.

I leaned forward to tap him on the shoulder. As he awoke and moved, the cot creaked under the strain. I knew one thing for sure: I wanted this monster on my side when the fighting started. He opened one blue eye, which focused in on Chan.

"What's this gook doing in here?"

Chan jumped to his feet. He rambled off a series of insults, some of which included the biological background of the big redhead's parents, his speech, his looks, his odor, and his intelligence. Richard Chan had a vocabulary that was difficult for most Marines to keep up with.

But when the big redhead opened both eyes, I knew that he had kept up with Chan's rant. Then a friendly smile appeared behind the large moustache. He laughed deep and strong, then stuck out his hand. Chan hesitated for an instant before he shook it.

"My name is Red. They call me Big Red. You look like boots."

"We are," I said. "Just got in today."

"What platoon are you in?" He rolled back to a comfortable position.

"Second Platoon," Chan said. "First Battalion, Fifth Marines."

"That means you're with me. What's your MOS?"

"Our Military Occupational Specialty is 0331." Chan's reply sounded like a line in a text book.

Red's smile stretched wider.

"Both gunners? Oh boy, they're sure going to be glad to see you two."

"Why is that?" asked Chan.

"I'm a gunner too," he said. "I got hit on the first day of Operation Hue City, and when I left, I was the last gunner with machine-gun MOS in the whole company. They were grabbing guys from mortars and guys from supply and sticking M60's in their hands, and believe me, they don't like humpin' through the bush with that bullet magnet. Do you remember that crap they told you in machine-gun school about the life expectancy of a gunner after a firefight begins?"

We nodded in unison.

"Well, they meant it. Seven to ten seconds. Don't get too worried, though," Red said, "I heard we might invade. If they let us go on offense, this war will be over in a few weeks." With that the big Marine rolled over to go back to sleep.

I knew he meant well, but he had just planted a seed of doubt that was growing into a tree. I tapped him on the shoulder again and felt like one of the little people waking up Gulliver. "Hey, you weren't kidding just a little, were you?" I asked quietly. "I mean, we can't be the only three gunners in all of Alpha Company."

"We are unless they got some more boots while I was in the hospital." He opened his eyes again. "Look, don't worry about it, 'cause it won't help. Find a salt when you get to your squad and stick with him like glue. If you don't get killed the first couple of months, you'll be okay."

"What should we do to get ready? Is there anything we should know?"

He looked us up and down before answering.

"You probably 'oughta take your dog tags off the chain. They make noise at night, and that noise'll get you killed. If your head gets blown off, they probably won't find the tags and you won't be identified. String 'em into your boot laces so they can't make noise. The boots usually hold together even if you hit a trip wire. And color 'em with something so they won't shine with the sunlight or moonlight. If you got anything you want to keep dry, put it in plastic and stick it between your helmet and helmet liner." He pointed at the grenades lying on my cot. "Bend the pin on those frags right now. When you hump through the bush, sticks get caught in the ring and pull out the pin. That's a rough way to get blown away."

Red's advice made me realize for the first time all of the assorted ways I could get myself killed in this place.

"Don't ever take your boots off unless you're in some area like Phu Bai. Put your crap-paper in plastic—writing paper too. If you don't put Halazone tablets in each canteen of water you'll get dysentery with the first drink. When it's 120 degrees, you'll drink a lot of water. And there ain't no stopping for head-calls when you got the runs all day and all night, so you just drain while you hump. Take your malaria pills every day or you'll get malaria and it'll stay with you even if you make it home. The salt tabs, too. Forget your salt tab and you'll pass out from heat exhaustion, and the lieutenant will wanna kill you 'cause it's the same as taking care of wounded. Medevacs can cost Marine lives. And take your helmet off when you get the chance. I saw one boot get his brain fried 'cause he left that steel pot on all day when it was a 120 degrees. Ask whoever is writing you to send care packages with Kool-Aid and stuff that won't spoil in the heat."

I felt like I was cramming for the biggest exam I ever had in high school. The Corps were professional killers, and our training was serious, but some of this we were hearing for the first time.

He pointed at Chan's M16 rifle. "Clean that Mattey Matel every day or it will jam."

"The M16?" Chan asked. "They told us this was the finest weapon in Vietnam."

"It's a piece of plastic crap! It jams constantly if you don't keep it spit-shined."

"What about the 'Sixty'?"

"It's the best weapon in Nam. Every Marine in the platoon depends on that Sixty. It can't jam or Marines die. During the monsoon season, your weapon will start to rust every few hours. Keep the gas cylinder clean and try to keep the mud out of your ammo belts."

Red went on with a list of ways to get yourself or the men around you killed, and it was frightening. But what Red said at the end of this terrifying list seemed to be the single most important item for us to live or die by as machine gunners.

"For you two, there is one thing more important than anything else. When you hear the call, 'Guns Up!', you got to get that gun to the point of contact and open up or Marines are gonna' die. Twenty-round burst. If you lay on that trigger for longer, your tracer rounds are a golden arrow pointing straight at your head, and every single enemy soldier is taught the same thing they taught us. Knock out the gun first. You will be the only visible target at night, and all enemy fire is gonna be directed right at you." He gave a laugh that had no joy to it, then ended his little speech the only way he could. "Semper fi, Marines."

That night, I pulled out my little Gideon Bible and read and prayed. When I was a kid, praying was part of my everyday life. They were simple kid prayers, but prayers nonetheless. By the time I turned fourteen, my mind was on anything but God. I still talked to Him, but He wasn't a priority. That was about to change.

* * * * *

We soon discovered that Red had not been exaggerating about the life expectancy of a "0331" in the 5th Marines. I became Red's A-gunner, the Marine that feeds belts of ammo into the machine gun. Chan went with another gun team. A gun team was supposed to have four or even five guys, but casualties to machine gunners was so high that we rarely, if ever, had more than two men, a gunner and an A-gunner. There were a few times when I was the entire machine gun team.

Shortly after we got to Nam, the platoon was sent to Truoi Bridge. It looked like an old train bridge back in the states, metal with concrete pillars. It was an important bridge on Highway One, the main supply route from Da Nang to Phu Bai to Hue City and all the way to the DMZ , the border with North Vietnam.

The NVA, North Vietnamese Army, overran the bridge with more than 400 men. Fifteen Marines died defending that bridge. Sappers, suicide squads, finally crawled out onto the bridge then blew it and themselves up. Big Red fired his M60 until he melted the barrel and started in on another one. His gun position came under relentless attack from B40 Rockets, mortars, rifles, and enemy .30 caliber machine guns. When most men would have kept their heads down, Red kept firing. I know that he saved a lot of Marines.

There were sixty-four confirmed dead NVA, but they dragged away many more dead and wounded. Thirty years after the battle, Red got the Bronze Star with combat V for valor. The Corps was never real generous at handing out medals, and it wasn't uncommon to hear some old salt remind us that no one joins the Corps for money, education, or medals: we joined to fight and to call ourselves Marines. And so we did.

3

KILLER TEAM

The NVA and Vietcong had death squads. Their job was to go into villages and murder members of the village chief's family if he did not supply the communists with rice and other supplies. Sometimes they would murder the village chief, cut off his head, and put it on a bamboo pole on the path leading into the village. It was all part of the communist/socialist way of getting the South Vietnamese people to embrace total government rule.

Of course, these small death squads only came into a village at night. We didn't combat these small squads of murderers with platoons of Marines. The Corps' strategy to fight these cowards was three-man killer teams.

Scuttlebutt was that a death squad was going to hit the village outside of Truoi Bridge. The Gunny had asked for volunteers for a Three-Man Killer Team, and since I had not actually been in the "bush" yet, I foolishly volunteered.

Two days later, I was at my usual task of filling sandbags and rebuilding bunker positions around the blown-up bridge when Big Red came my way. There was a Marine named Striker filling bags with me. He was an unfriendly character with an ugly attitude, but he was a tough Marine.

"You two are going out on a killer team tonight with Jackson," Red said. "Clark's a boot, so let's go over a couple things. Once you set up, bend the pins on your frags so they're ready to use. Lay out a couple of clips to reload quickly."

"Clark, the gooks can smell bug juice, so if there's any breeze you can't use it." Striker's tone was friendly enough but filled with concern as they both made sure I was ready for this.

Red added, "And don't take your poncho, either. The gooks can hear the rain bouncing off it. Leave your helmet here, too. Wear your soft cover."

My stomach started to tighten up. This was beginning to seem more dangerous than I was prepared for.

"If you guys see the trip flares go off and the bridge is getting hit," Red said, "don't come back in. Stay where you are until daybreak." Now I felt really nervous.

A thousand years later, the sun finally began to drop behind the faraway mountains of the A Shau Valley. My stomach churned like an abdominal alarm clock. I met Jackson and Striker at the gun bunker on the south end of the bridge. Jackson had taped two magazine clips together end to end for quick reloading. I immediately wished that someone had told me to do that. It seemed like there was always one more thing I didn't know or never thought of. I knew it would probably be that one more thing that would get me killed.

As we started down the path through the village, two Marines dragged rolls of concertina wire across the road, sealing the bridge for the night. Seeing that gave me an uneasy sensation of being completely alone. Filling sandbags suddenly seemed like a lovely way to spend my time in Nam.

We walked through the village unnoticed—
we hoped. The villagers slept in small underground
bunkers usually beside their huts or under the hut.
It was hard to imagine what that must be like,
having to sleep in dark damp holes so much of the
time. Except for the occasional coughing from one
of the hole-dwellers, the only other sounds came
from the river. The splash of a fish made me bite
my tongue.

At the end of the village, the path split in
three directions. Jackson held up his hand for us to
halt. We knelt on one knee.

Timing was crucial for any ambush. If we
set up too early, we might be seen; but if we
waited too long, we might choose a bad spot or
walk into an enemy ambush. I strained to make out
any movement up ahead, but I couldn't see beans.

Jackson motioned to move out. Every step
sounded too loud. The safety of the bridge felt a
million miles away. I kept looking behind me, but
the only thing following was my own fear. Jackson
took a path that led away from the river.

Our pace slowed to one quiet step at a time.
A branch fell to our right and splashed into the
river. We all dropped to one knee. I could see no
sane reason for going one more step away from the

bridge. Jackson stood up. He motioned to move out again. I wanted to tell him that if all this had been designed to scare the new boot, not another step was needed. My knees were jelly.

I wanted somebody back home to know what I was going through. Right then, my friends were cruising around Steak 'n Shake trying to pick up women. This was crazy. No one back in St. Pete would ever believe this.

What was I supposed to do if I got hit?

I had to quit cluttering up my mind.

The deepening night steadily took any vision I had had at the start. I kept Striker in sight, but Jackson was part of the blackness ahead. I wanted to stop. We kept going. A woodsy noise behind me started my heart pounding. I turned and walked backward for twenty meters. The paranoia of being stalked from behind had me terrified. I turned back around. Now Striker was gone. The urge to call out his name got as far as my throat before I managed to control it. I started walking faster.

A quarter moon slipped out from behind a large thick cloud. The jungle blackness turned misty blue. It was like trying to see through a heavy fog, but it wasn't fog. It was just another eerie Vietnam night, dense with humidity. Now I could see Striker and Jackson.

Instead of feeling better, the dim blue light made me jittery. Suddenly I felt conspicuous. Sweat dripped into my eyes and stung them with salt. The path looked like it might lead all the way to the dreaded A Shau Mountains.

We finally stopped at the edge of a clearing about twenty-five meters square. The path led through its center and into thick jungle on the other side that appeared as a solid black wall. In the center of the clearing, another path crisscrossed ours. Most of the paths led to the rice paddies that the villagers worked each day, but some went through or around the paddy fields and all the way to the mountains.

The new path led in a direction away from the bridge, southwest, toward the A Shau Mountains. The men always joked about that area being a gook R&R center. It didn't seem very funny right now. Jackson knelt down on one knee. He motioned for us to do the same.

"This is it," he whispered.

"How about over there, behind those bushes?" Striker pointed to some knee-high shrubs ten feet from where the two paths crossed. It looked like a logical place but was well into the clearing and rather naked.

"I'll go first and check it out," Jackson whispered.

"Make sure we're hidden from both paths," added Striker.

Jackson crouched as he scampered into the clearing. His boots rushing through the foot-high sawgrass made too much noise. He disappeared behind the bushes for a moment then raised one hand and motioned for us to follow.

Striker went first. He made too much noise too. Once Striker had ducked out of sight, I followed. My first few steps were quiet but slow. Then I ran for the cover of the bushes, making more noise than both of them.

We set up three feet away from each other. Our cover was perfect for watching the paths without being seen. I tried to remember all the things I'd been taught, but all I could focus on was the merciless attack of gigantic mosquitoes. Jackson gave Striker a bottle of insect repellant. Striker put some on his face, neck, and hands, and then leaned toward me.

"Put some on, but not too heavy. The gooks can smell it if the wind is right."

Jackson leaned over and handed me a watch with the face down.

"You got first watch. Don't let the luminous hands show or we're all dead." Jackson smiled. His smile was more luminous than any watch. "Wake Striker at 2400 hours."

As soon as they closed their eyes I felt like I was the only target in Vietnam. Every bush and every tree began looking like an enemy soldier. I tried to calm down by thinking how miserable I felt. It was no use. I was too excited to be miserable.

The quarter moon slid in and out of occasional clouds, seesawing visibility from ten feet to three hundred. Between each lapse in visibility, trees and bushes seemed to move. All the John Wayne war movies I'd ever seen began to haunt me. The Japs always disguised themselves as bushes. I started to wake Striker up, but I didn't. The Vietnamese had probably never even seen a John Wayne movie.

Jackson and Striker had pulled their shirts up and retracted their heads like turtles in an effort to evade the constant whining of mosquitoes. I checked the watch. Only twenty-five minutes had gone by. It felt like twenty-five days, but so far so good. Not a single bush had snuck up on me yet. Maybe the night would go by without incident.

One more scan of the clearing dispelled that hope. The shadowy figure of a man slowly emerged from the jungle like a ghost, crouching as he cautiously moved forward, step by step. My heart thumped so strongly I could feel my chest moving.

I clicked my rifle off safety and felt for my spare magazines.

Striker slapped at a mosquito. I quickly put my hand over his mouth. He froze stiff, his eyes opened wide.

"Gooks," I whispered so low I wasn't sure he heard me. I quietly rolled toward Jackson and gave him a nudge on the shoulder. They both looked at me. I pointed at the shadow. They both came up on their left elbows and peaked over the brush that hid us. Three shadows were now visible leaving the thick jungle and proceeding across the clearing. They weren't on either of the trails. They were coming straight at us. We took aim. Fifteen meters away they veered slightly away from us. Now a large group of shadows appeared at the edge of the clearing. We held our fire.

My eyebrows were back to my hairline. I could see at least forty shadows moving into the clearing. Jackson motioned for us to get down. The faint whisper of an aircraft overhead stole my mind, and for an instant, I prayed to be on that plane, or any plane. I then prayed for something more sensible. I asked God to save us.

I melted myself into the ground and prayed silently, *"Yea though I walk through the valley . . ." Oh, God forgive me, I can't remember the words!*

The rustle of feet swishing through damp sawgrass pounded into my ears. If one man stepped a couple of feet to his left, we were dead and we each knew it.

It became frighteningly obvious that this was at least a full company of 120 NVA. I could literally smell their sweat, and they reeked of fish and rice and maybe garlic. It was dark but not that dark. It was impossible that not one man out of a 120 hyper alert men had seen us or stepped on us. That they didn't was absolutely the power of God and as incredible as this miracle was, it still doesn't compare to the miracle the Lord gave me on Graybeard Mountain many years later.

Suddenly, we heard the booming of heavy artillery in the distance, probably out of Phu Bai. Thirty seconds later, two rounds exploded about a thousand meters away, judging by the sound. The Ho-chi-minh sandals began moving faster by my face.

I wanted Big Red to be here. Flashbacks of boot camp blended with the fear. One slap of a mosquito and my life was over. One sneeze. One ill-timed twitch.

My mind went everywhere. I remembered when a recruit slapped a sand flea in front of me at Parris Island. The DI kicked him in the shins and knocked him down. Then he made the whole platoon lie down, and he screamed at the top of his lungs, "Private, you have just killed my entire platoon!"

My arm was aching like crazy, but I didn't dare move even my eyes to see why. I could hear the enemy huffing and grunting as they filed by. I could feel each second individually. I felt like I'd spent days lying here with my face in the mud.

Finally, silence. No more feet shuffling by. I wanted to look up. Suddenly gripping terror seized my mind. The gooks were standing over us. They

40

would shoot me in the head when I looked up. Two minutes passed.

"All clear." To me Jackson's whisper was a loud choir singing, "Hal-le-lu-jah." Somewhere, bells were ringing, and the sun would come up tomorrow.

I looked straight into Striker's eyes. He had a tourniquet grip on my arm.

"My trousers are wet," he said as he released me. "And it ain't rainin'."

My back hurt, my legs were numb, and the blood still wasn't back in my arm. My neck cracked, and then it felt better. Then it hit me. It grabbed my funny bone and squeezed it just like Striker had been squeezing my arm for the last eternity.

"Your trousers are wet?" I looked into Striker's muddy face. He nodded yes. It started with a snicker, then grew into a contained laugh, then out of control. I laughed so hard I snorted. Tears of sheer delight gushed uncontrollably down my muddy face. Jackson leaned over and shook my shoulder.

"Don't . . ." His warning turned into a chuckle. Then Striker began laughing. I covered my mouth with my arm to hide the noise, but it only made me laugh harder. It was like trying not to laugh in church or at a funeral. Jackson's chuckle grew louder. Smilin' Jackson could laugh louder and harder than anyone I'd ever met. I felt an urgency to quiet him down before he got going, but it was no use. I was out of control. Jackson rolled onto his back, his knees pulled into his stomach as if he were in great pain, and laughed. Great, big, fat, from-the-pit-of-his-stomach belly laughs.

Jackson sat up in panic.

"Oh, God! Grenade!"

In the span of two seconds we crawled, hopped, and ran ten meters away. We were hugging the ground again when the grenade went off, spitting dirt all over us. Striker and I sat up immediately after the explosion with rifles at the ready.

Jackson chuckled.

We stared at him in disbelief. Jackson's chuckle turned into a cackle. Striker shook Jackson by his shoulder, which only made him laugh harder and louder.

"If you don't stop, I'm going to butt-stroke you," Striker growled.

"Okay, okay," Jackson replied, the words squeezing between snickers. "It was my grenade. I pulled the pin when the gooks were walking by."

"We better get out of here!" I said, trying to keep my panic to a whisper.

"They won't turn that big column around. They'll just think somebody tripped a booby-trap."

"Just the same," Striker whispered with a quick look around, "let's get out of here. We might not get another miracle."

He was absolutely right. It had been a miracle. It was as though God had made us invisible to an entire company of NVA soldiers. We each knew that we should be dead and that only God could have kept all those NVAs from seeing us or stumbling over us. I thanked Him all night long and couldn't wait to write a letter back home to tell somebody what happened, even if they wouldn't believe it.

We were waiting outside the concertina wire blocking Highway One when it was pulled back. We made our way across the blown-up bridge to the Marine compound, and it felt as safe as being back home in St. Pete. It seemed pretty weird when a bridge that's just been overrun by more than 400 enemy troops feels safe, but it was true.

The bush was a very scary place. I didn't even get to sit down before the Gunny yelled, "Saddle up!" My long nightmare in the jungles and mountains of Vietnam had begun.

PFC JOHNNIE CLARK

4

THE GIDEON AND RED

One day we set up a on a barren hill that looked like every other barren hill in Nam. My pack straps had worn grooves into my flak jacket, which had worn grooves into my shoulders, and I wanted that weight off me as quickly as possible. The Gunny decided on the perfect spot for the gun team, and it looked like home. I carried four-hundred rounds of machine gun ammo that I had to drop before I could get that pack off me.

The pack had barely hit the ground when I heard a thumping sound in the distance. The second hollow thumping sound of a mortar leaving the tube echoed across the hilltop, bringing a wave of quiet over the chattering Marines. Some men looked up while others flattened against the rocky surface of the hill.

The first round hit twenty yards away. I tried to crawl under my helmet. It was about as helpless as I had ever felt in my life. All anyone could do was wait and see if the next round was the last thing you were going to hear. The second explosion shook the ground, and someone started screaming in agony. After a third explosion somebody yelled, "Guns Up! Guns Up!"

Big Red punched me in the shoulder as he got to his feet with the M60 and a couple of hundred round belts. I pushed to my feet with my M16 and two more belts of ammo. In an instant we were sprinting up and over the crest of the hill as mortar rounds continued to explode around the perimeter. I heard myself screaming, "Yeee-haw!" like some drunken cowboy as we made a mad dash to where, I didn't know, while everyone else was flattened out.

Then I saw the lieutenant up ahead pointing toward another hill about a hundred meters south. Red hit the dirt and opened up on the hill. As quickly as it had started, it stopped. The mortars ceased. A few minutes later, a Marine Huey helicopter appeared and started strafing the other side of the enemy hill. We heard later that they killed that mortar team.

The corpsman was treating a guy who was pretty badly hurt as I made my way back to our position. That's when I saw one of the guys holding what was left of my pack and laughing. It was shredded to pieces, and so was everything I owned.

Red slapped me on the back. "Don't worry. Our packs suck anyway. I'll get you an NVA pack like mine next time we get some confirmed."

It was at that moment that I felt a sharp burning pain high on my right thigh. I bent over.

"What's wrong with you?" Red asked.

"I don't know." I felt a warm trickle of blood running down my leg. Two small holes in my trousers near the groin were the only evidence I needed.

"Red! I'm wounded. I've been hit!"

"What? Where?" Red dropped the M60 and in a flash he was kneeling in front of me.

"Unbutton your trousers, stupid! Let's see how bad it is."

"I wonder why I didn't feel it sooner?"

"Happens that way sometimes."

"Wow! My own little red badge of courage! I read that book in my English class."

"This could have been real tough on your love life, boot. Are you hit anywhere else?"

"Will I get a Purple Heart?"

"Are you sure you aren't hit anywhere else? What's this?" He pointed to a tear in my left chest pocket. "What's in that pocket?"

I unbuttoned the flap over my pocket and pulled my small Gideon Bible out. It was wrapped in plastic to keep it dry, and there was a hole in the plastic. I unwrapped it and stared at a hole right under the word "Holy." It sent a stream of goose bumps down to my toes. The hole didn't go all the way through the little Bible, but it went far enough to have left a lifelong impact on me. A splinter of very sharp shrapnel was wedged inside the little book. I looked at Red, who seemed to be in deep thought as he stared at that Gideon.

"Could that have killed me, Red?"

"We had a guy killed by a sliver no bigger than that. It took us an hour to find out what killed him. A sliver of shrapnel smaller than that had gone just under his helmet in the back. Didn't bleed much and it was in his hair, so we couldn't see it. Went into his brain."

We sat down and waited for the corpsman to finish working on the Marine who was badly wounded. We both stared at that Bible, and I read out of the page where the shrapnel stopped. I don't remember what the verse was, but I think it was out of *Hebrews* and about faith.

Red was moved by what had happened, too. We talked about the Bible and God, and I guess I tried to be a witness. Red wanted to know God, that was clear. From that day on, I felt even closer to Big Red. We both thought that we had witnessed a miracle.

I was pretty hyped, and maybe there are a thousand stories about Bibles stopping shrapnel, but when that Bible is over your heart and you're the one living it, it's not something you ever forget. That being said, compared to what God did on Graybeard Mountain, shrapnel in my Bible barely registers.

A little later Doc, our corpsman, tweezered out the two splinters of shrapnel in me and laughed when I asked about a Purple Heart. As soon as the medevac lifted off with the wounded Marine, somebody yelled, "Saddle up!"

I got the wounded guy's pack.

* * * * *

I had been in Nam long enough to lose a lot of weight, and though I was no longer a boot, I was no "old salt" either. It was May 19 when Red pulled me to my feet and helped me get my pack and gun ammo back on after another ambush. He was like the big brother I never had, and if anyone in Nam was my security blanket, it was Red.

The terrain turned hard and hilly with little vegetation. At 1900 hours, the seventeen-man column stopped. We dropped to one knee and waited to be placed in ambush position. We had a full blooded American Indian in our platoon, Corporal Swift Eagle. Chan and I didn't believe anyone could have a name that was that cool until he showed us his dog-tags. He was a deadly Marine and I was glad the guy was on our side. Swift Eagle and Gunny Mac swept through the column taking three men at a time and quickly placing them in position for the night. When they finished, we had a textbook L-shaped ambush.

It was that eerie time of the day. The lighting was just right for your eyes to play tricks on you. A pinkish yellow twilight filtered across the brown-and-green earth, casting odd shadows that made me nervous.

Tactically, we were on our own except for possible artillery support from Phu Bai, about five miles north. There was supposed to be an enemy battalion out here roaming around. The logic of sending seventeen Marines to make contact with an NVA battalion had escaped me, but I was only a private first class. I was contemplating the prospects of finding an NVA battalion when Red woke me up with a stiff elbow to the shoulder.

"Do you see movement?"

"Where?" I asked.

"Straight ahead. Keep looking straight ahead."

I strained to see what he was aiming at. Then I saw movement. Shadowy figures silhouetted by evaporating sunlight looked to be moving thirty meters away. I felt myself trying to crouch lower as I took aim. I covered my mouth and whispered in the direction of the Marines on my left.

"Gooks!"

I started linking up ammo for the gun. Suddenly green tracers shot across our position from the left flank. Then another burst of fire came at us from straight ahead. Seven khaki-clad NVA appeared from the shadows in front of us. They were led by an officer who suddenly ran toward us firing a pistol. The others carried AKs. They looked surprised, maybe as surprised as we were. A couple turned and ran from us, but the others followed their leader. Red opened up first, making us the only target they had. The officer was lifted off his feet and blown backward with the first twenty rounds. The gun stopped firing. I started firing my M16, but the targets disappeared. All firing ceased. I knew Red was hit. I could feel blood, and it wasn't mine. He was slumped forward onto the gun.

I could hear myself calling for a corpsman. My voice sounded dreamlike. For an instant I thought I was dreaming. I thought I'd wake up and find that none of this really happened. Swift Eagle flattened out beside me. He looked at the back of Red's head with no expression.

Doc slid in beside us, breathing hard.

"He's dead, Doc," Swift Eagle said.

"Red?" Doc asked.

"Yeah. Put his poncho over him. I'll get an A-gunner for the boot."

"He only had a month to go." Doc's voice sounded far away.

The night crept by sleeplessly, congested with weird, fully awake dreams of home, friends, and the Marine Corps. I felt numb. It started drizzling. The sound always reminded me of French fries in a pan.

At first light, it was still raining. The air smelled fresh and crisp. It was a stateside rain, not the normal pounding rain of a monsoon, which sounds more like a war than the war itself. Raindrops formed tiny puddles on Red's poncho. His huge Viking boots stuck out of the poncho as if from a blanket that was too small. I was thankful for the rain. It kept away the ants and flies and hid my tears. How could he be dead? Men like that couldn't just die. He told me if you got past the first two months, you'd make it.

I wanted to pray; I needed God now. I felt like I had not been close to the Lord since I was fourteen and hit high school, but prayer had always been a part of my life. Listening to my Dad pray and talk to God when he thought he was alone was a life lesson that stayed with me even when the rest of my life was a selfish mess.

I remembered the gunny's warning that I couldn't be eighteen anymore, that I had to grow up right now. I looked around again, and the lieutenant was walking my way. His young Annapolis face couldn't hide the loss. No tears, but he was frowning with pain. He pulled back the poncho, grimaced, and covered him again.

"You're the gunner now, Marine. Keep it clean. Every man here depends on it. Red said you'd do all right. Don't let him down." His words sounded rehearsed.

"I won't."

"Look, Marine, I don't know what to say. I thought the world of that big redhead. You've been dropped into a real tough spot. I'm here to help in any way I can. If you have questions, I want you to come to me. If I don't know the answers, we'll go to the chief or the gunny or whatever it takes. Do you pray?" he asked bluntly.

"Yes, sir," I said, surprised at the question.

"Start praying, John. He'll get us through this mess." He walked away.

The clapping sound of a chopper was approaching. I watched the radioman, throw out a green smoke grenade. A few minutes later, I helped carry Red's body up the ramp of a supply chopper. We laid him down easy, and I walked back to the gun in a daze and sat in the mud.

"Johnnie." I pulled my eyes off the M60.

Cpl. Bob Carrol, the radioman, stood over me. "Here." He threw me Red's NVA pack; it was empty. "Take this, too." He tossed me Red's .45-caliber pistol and holster. "You're the gunner now, right?"

"Yeah, I'm the gunner."

And the gunny had been right. I was eighteen but I would never be young again.

5

COMING HOME IN THE MIDNIGHT HOUR

When my war was over, I came home to an ungrateful nation that had been lied to by the liberal media. America didn't seem to know the good guys from the bad guys any more. Soldiers had witnessed up close just exactly what the communists were. When they invaded Hue City, they killed everyone who worked for the government, from school teachers to mailmen. They murdered many in a Catholic school and preferred bayoneting people to death to save ammo. Death squads murdered over forty thousand people, and most were just villagers who wanted their own rice to feed their own families.

I was cheering along with the other men as the big C-130 touched down at El Torro Marine Air Base in California. A lot of the Marines had been badly wounded and some crippled for life, so the healthy guys helped the men who couldn't walk. I pushed a kid off who had no legs. There was a red carpet and a small Marine band playing our hymn. A group of ladies had set up a stand with lemonade and cookies at the end of the red carpet at a small terminal entrance.

About twenty yards to our right was a tall chain link fence. Most of us didn't notice right away, but a group of war protesters were on the other side of that fence, and a platoon of Marine MP's were standing with their backs to these people on our side.

The protesters were screaming "baby killers" and holding up some really foul signs. A few were mooning us. At first I was sort of confused as to what they were doing, but I think that when that first tomato hit the ground near me, when the egg splattered on the Marine's wheelchair, my rage started.

I ran toward the fence with some of the other Marines. There was going to be bloodshed. I truly wanted to kill these scumbags. We quickly discovered that the platoon of MP's were not there to protect us but were there to protect these cowards from us.

I was healthy. As a matter of fact, maybe I was a little more than healthy physically. I had been in Japan and Okinawa for months rehabbing from bullet wounds. Part of my rehab was training in martial arts. The Marines that trained in Okinawa fully expected to go back to Nam, so we were not training to win championship belts or trophies: we were training to kill someone in hand-to-hand combat. Martial arts would end up being my profession for the next forty-five years, and my practice was a way to contain my anger.

They gave us forty-eight hours leave for the guys who could travel. Another Marine, who was from California, and I caught a cab for the nearest bar. We wanted a cold American beer. When we reached town and started roaming the streets, it was like seeing civilization for the first time. I had been in Japan and Okinawa rehabbing, so I wasn't coming straight from the jungle, but it was still quite a thrill—until we found our first bar. On the door was a sign in big letters that read, "No Dogs Or Marines Allowed In Bar"

I was angry and confused and wanted to fight, but my buddy pulled me away. "Let's just find another bar."

When we found a second bar with a similar sign, I kicked the front door. No one came out, and it's a good thing for everyone that they didn't. My buddy told me that we needed to go to his home town. It wasn't like LA, and we could have a home-cooked meal. His mom didn't know he was home yet, and he wanted to surprise her. That sounded great.

We found the Los Angeles Greyhound Bus terminal, and my friend was asking a teller about bus routes and costs. I was watching two cops arresting an old drunk on the other side of the terminal when two hippie-looking guys came up to me. One had long hair and a head band. The other had Army fatigues with peace signs sewn on the shoulders.

"Hey, Marine, would you like to come over to our pad for a couple of ice cold beers?"

"Yeah! That sounds great!"

I turned to face my buddy, who was walking toward me. "These guys just invited us over for cold beers."

In spite of all I had seen, I was still very naïve. When my buddy gave me a funny look and told me they were homosexuals, I felt like an idiot and told them to go away. One of them called me a baby killer and spit on my uniform, so I naturally decked him. The other one ran away yelling for help.

The police dropped the wino they were arresting, and a few minutes later I was being handcuffed. They threw my seabag in the trunk of their cruiser and put me in the back seat. I guess my friend went on to his home town. I never saw him again.

The cops drove me a couple of blocks away and pulled up to a bus stop. One had been looking at me in the rear view mirror. He spoke without turning around.

"Fifth Marines, huh."

I knew right away I was going to be okay. The Fifth and Sixth Marines were the only Regiments allowed to wear the French Fourragère. It had been given to the Fifth Marine Regiment for saving Paris in WWI. Only a Marine would know that.

"Yeah," I said. "Alpha One Five."

"We were in Fox Two Five."

I wanted to shout for joy. The cop on the passenger side got out of the car and opened the back door. He took off the cuffs while the other cop retrieved my seabag from the trunk. The cop with my seabag set it down beside me. He looked at the ribbons on my dress greens.

"You've seen a lot of crap, jarhead. Just get back?"

"Twenty-four hours," I said.

"You sit here and wait for bus number thirty-four. It'll take you back to El Torro."

"That guy spit on my uniform."

"Yeah, we know, Marine. It ain't gonna get any easier. Just don't deck 'em in front of cops, you idiot."

With that, they got back in the squad car and drove away with casual salutes. Little did I know how right those cops would be. A few days later, I was discharged and on a Delta Air Lines flight heading to Atlanta and on to Tampa. I tried to fall asleep, but I was realizing that sleep would never be the same for me. I seemed to always be slightly awake and slightly ready to fight.

I could feel the eyes of someone on me and jerked awake to face them. It was a woman around forty years old. She was well dressed and fairly attractive. She smiled an unpleasant smile and pointed at the ribbons on my uniform.

"Are you some sort of hero?"

I was caught a little off guard. "No, ma'am. Just a Marine."

She pointed again. "So the little gold stars on that one? Is that for killing more women and children than the average Marine?"

It's hard to explain or describe the surprise I felt. I think I just couldn't believe she actually said that. I stared at her for a moment and could feel the blood rushing to my face. I couldn't hit a woman, but I had never wanted to hit anyone any more than I wanted to hit her. She said something else, but I could only see her mouth moving because rage was filling my ears, too, and I couldn't hear a word.

At that moment, a beautiful Delta stewardess unsnapped the lady's seat belt and took her hand. "You're moving to another seat, madam."

The woman was in shock, mouth open, indignant. "I will do no such thing."

"Yes, you will and right now, or I will have you forcibly removed. Now get up."

The lady moved to another seat as she threatened everyone's job on the way to the back of the plane. The beautiful stewardess reappeared. She leaned over and said, "Welcome home, Marine. Your drinks are on Delta Air Lines. What'll you have?"

I'd be a liar if I didn't admit that that stewardess made the incident almost worth it. She invited me to stay the night in Atlanta with her and, once again, I'd be a liar if I didn't say I've always thought about what might have been. But my mom and my Uncle Bobby were waiting at the airport in Tampa for me. Bobby was an old Marine and had flown in from Virginia just for the night to greet me home. I couldn't blow him off, but it was close.

Mom and Paul, Uncle Bobby, and one of my best friends, Ben Allen, greeted me in Tampa that night. Not a ticker-tape parade, but no one threw tomatoes.

My poor mom had been through hell. Soldiers had come to her front door when Howard had been killed in action in 1945. So each time Marines brought her a telegram informing her I had been wounded she suffered. Paul told me that she had a little breakdown, but the old country girl was tough. She could take an awful lot.

My first morning home, mom jumped on my bed to hug and kiss me. In an instant I had thrown her to the floor and was choking her out. If Uncle Bobby hadn't jumped on me and gotten me off her, I don't want to think what I could have done. God had him there for that reason.

Watching the nightly news made me sick and angry. They were liars, and only the guys who'd been there knew it. America was drinking the Kool-Aid and believing everything people like Walter Cronkite and Jane Fonda had to say. Fitting in to a society that rejected me was difficult. I was very angry. A peace sign on a bumper was all I needed to start a fight. It was not uncommon for me to remove bumper stickers and threaten the owners. When a hippie walked into a hamburger joint wearing a dress green Marine Corps blouse with sergeant chevrons, I convinced him to take it off. The management called the police, but it was over by the time they arrived. I think I left with his coat.

I couldn't sleep without a gun and my KA-BAR, that's a combat knife Marines carry. I wrote a few books full of explanations to explain my habit, but one ambush stands out, and I want to tell you about it because it plays a role in my life and even mattered a little on Graybeard Mountain.

* * * * *

It was June in Thua Thien Province not far from the A Shau Valley. Marines are the best disciplined, toughest fighting outfit in the world. I know there's a lot of talk about "special" forces these days, but Marines are usually the men who are sent to rescue those "special" forces. But that's another story, and I've already written a couple of books about those things.

The point is that even the battle-hardened Marines I served with had limits. We didn't visit a war zone for a weekend and fly back to a base and a bed somewhere. For us, war was twenty-four hours a day, day after day, week after week, month after month.

We had been going for weeks, humping the mountains all day and setting up ambushes all night. Days of humping through the most vicious terrain on earth with the weight of packs, canteens, flak-jackets, helmets, twenty-four-pound machine guns, and four hundred rounds of ammo, not to mention grenades, pistols and KA-BAR brought on bone aching fatigue. Nights of waiting perfectly still while being sucked dry by mosquitoes and leeches and straining to see or hear the slightest movement. Then, when that movement finally appeared, there was terror and combat. Hours later it all started again.

Red had been killed, and Chan was back from a month at China Beach, where he'd been sent to learn Vietnamese. He was my A-gunner, and I was really happy to have him. Each night we tried to sleep in two-hour shifts. More than once we got the whispered word to "saddle up" in the middle of the night. That usually was the start of an all-night hump that sometimes meant crossing rivers or over mountains or through jungles that shredded your utilities, clothes to civilians, along with any exposed skin.

Staying alert twenty-four hours a day for months is not humanly possible, but the Corps didn't seem to care. We all complained, which was our right as Marines, and there was always some old salt who would ask you why didn't you join the Navy. This was especially enjoyable when our corpsman complained because he did join the Navy and still got stuck with the Marines.

One night as we walked along a small footpath on the side of a hill, the guy in front of me held up his hand and went to one knee. The whispered word came back to set in, to ambush the trail. Soon, Chan and I were placed below the trail to cover anything coming up the hill. It made no sense. The gun should have been ambushing the trail, but we were all too exhausted to think clearly or to care anymore.

I took the first watch as Chan pulled off four hundred rounds of machine gun ammo, his pack, and his flak-jacket. He used his pack as a pillow and fell asleep immediately. Mosquitoes were sucking the life out of me, so I pulled my poncho up around me until all that showed were my bloodshot eyes. A few moments later, I was falling forward asleep but jerked awake again. I pulled the stock of the M60 up into my gut so if I fell forward asleep, it would wake me.

I still nodded off, each time jerking awake so scared I couldn't breathe. It wasn't just fear of the enemy sneaking up on me, it was also fear that friggin' Indian, Corporal Swift Eagle would sneak up behind me and cut me with a KA-BAR knife. That was his way of making sure no one fell asleep on an ambush. But even the fear of Corporal Swift

Eagle could not overcome the absolute exhaustion. I was half awake and half asleep and having weird dreams of home and cruising around Steak & Shake trying to pick up girls. At one point, I could even hear the radio playing my favorite band, The Young Rascals. They were singing "In The Midnight Hour."

My eyes opened. I stiffened, frozen in a state of utter disbelief. We had not heard a radio or American music in months. Now, in the middle of a black night in the bush of Nam, I was hearing The Young Rascals blaring. My mind was totally confused, and my body was shocked stiff but ready.

Suddenly the sounds of an M14 opened fire from behind and above me. The rounds were coming down on our machine gun position, and my ears and face stung as bullets slapped through the poncho I had wrapped over my head. I should have been killed.

A moment later, the music rushed at me from behind, and then suddenly the weight of a man crashed into my back. We rolled downhill while I fought him and my poncho. Getting to my .45 was hopeless, but in that horrible few moments, I got to my KA-BAR.

It was just another night in the bush and one of a thousand reasons why I only half sleep, and I only half sleep with a KA-BAR and a gun to this day. It is also one of a thousand things that drove me to Graybeard Mountain and the most incredible day of my life.

6

DRUDGERY AND SPIDER HOLES

In 1970 I'd been home for about six months when the VA in St. Pete diagnosed me with mild combat fatigue. They gave me lots of pills, mostly Darvon and Valium. The Darvon was for wounds, while the Valium was to keep me calm and help me sleep. Of course, I shared my endless supply of pills with friends who wanted them. It seemed like the whole country, at least in my age group, was getting high on pills, pot, hash, acid, or just booze. Life was just one drunken party after another, always trying hopelessly to forget about Nam.

Some high school football buddies had a party at a house I was staying in. I went to bed a little early and a little drunk. I no longer fit in with my friends. We were the same age, but I was older than they were now. One of my close friends, a boy named Ben Allen, was at the party. Ben was the only friend to meet me at the airport when I came home.

My bedroom door was open. I thought I was asleep, but as always, I was never fully asleep. Ben was going to the bathroom, and his shadow went across my eyes. In an instant I was sitting up aiming my pistol. He was a twitch away from dead. It scared the crap out of Ben, but the truth is, I think it scared me more. I stopped sleeping with a gun for a few months and just slept with a KA-BAR. But it didn't last.

I needed a job. I'd made the mistake of swearing to God that I would never be in the mud again, and I'd never be around dead bodies again. Never tell God what you won't do.

71

My first job was laying telephone cable for a company named Burnip & Sims. When I wasn't using a jack-hammer to tear up streets, I was digging ditches in rain and mud. Of course, the rain wasn't as bad as it had been in Vietnam, and neither was the heat, but it was still rain and heat and mud.

One day I found myself in a huge trench that had been dug across 66th Street in St. Pete. Now, 66th Street is one of the busier streets in St. Petersburg. Detouring traffic on it was a big deal, so the company was in a hurry to get the job done. There was some problem with a main line at the bottom of that giant trench, and, for whatever reason, there I was in the middle of a downpour trying to fix that big black cable. They had tied a rope around me connected to a backhoe just in case of a cave-in.

Flashbacks are weird, and the silliest things can send me back to 'Nam. Sometimes, it's an odor, and sometimes it's the obvious sound of a chopper flying overhead. This time it was that rope.

* * * * *

We patrolled all day and set up ambushes all night. If there is a more miserable place on earth than Vietnam, I never want to see it. I never actually slept, not sleep as any normal person would clarify it. We were all hyper-alert—always straining to see a potential trip wire or an ambush in a black jungle.

After two months in the bush, I had lost twenty pounds and looked ten years older. I wondered what thirteen months would do to me. During one span of time, we made contact with the NVA nearly every day for more than two weeks. You rarely knew when it was coming or how, but each time someone yelled, "Guns Up!" my heart was in my throat and the adrenalin deafened me.

When the monsoons hit, our skin turned a sickly chalky color from being wet twenty-four hours a day. If we dug in and actually fell asleep, which usually only came from total exhaustion, it was common to wake up choking and near drowning. The leeches would get at any skin, exposed or unexposed. You never knew they were on you until they became heavy with your blood. If you freaked out and pulled them off, the head stayed under your skin, and the infection was awful. We burned them off of each other in the mornings when the light or odor of a match wouldn't give away our position and get us killed.

What blood the leeches didn't get, the swarms of incessant mosquitoes did. The snakes were either huge or tiny, but they were all deadly, like the Bamboo Viper. We called the little green viper a two-stepper. If it bit you, you took about two more steps and dropped. It seemed like everything in Vietnam was trying to kill us. The insects were huge, and I hated them, all of them. I really hated the spiders.

One day we came upon a Spider Hole that led to an underground tunnel. Corporal Swift Eagle was talking to the Lieutenant and pointing at me. Swift Eagle was one very tough Marine. If he caught a Marine asleep, he would snatch their head back and cut their throat with a KA-BAR knife. Not a deep cut, just enough to cause infection and scare a few years out of your life. I knew it wasn't a good sign when Swift Eagle walked over to me and slapped a .45 caliber pistol into my hand.

"Clark, you're going down in that tunnel to see what's there."

Next thing I knew they were tying a rope onto my right ankle.

"What's that for?" I asked.

"If you hit a trip wire or somethin', we can pull you out."

No one in the Corps seemed to care if I had claustrophobia, so a few minutes later I was squeezing into a gook spider hole on my stomach with a flashlight and a .45 caliber pistol. I started praying the twenty-third Psalm, but soon I was too scared to remember the words.

A few feet into the tunnel, it bent to the left. I don't know if a person could hate doing something much more than I hated doing that. I was having trouble breathing because there wasn't much air and because I was so scared, I was holding my breath. I was able to move forward on my elbows and the toes of my boots with the flashlight and the .45 pointing ahead. The tunnel started getting a little larger, but I couldn't quite come up on all fours.

I expected to come face to face with an NVA soldier at any second, and I knew the survivor would be whoever pulled the trigger first. The stench was suffocating, moldy and damp and rotten like the rest of Nam, only worse. Sweat poured from my forehead into my eyes, and they stung with salt, but I forced them as wide open as they would ever be. The only way I could keep the

.45 and the flashlight pointing straight ahead while moving forward was to pull my knees in until my butt hit the top of the tunnel and then slide forward on my elbows like a caterpillar.

It felt like I'd been down in that hole for hours, but it was probably only a few minutes. I pulled my knees in until my butt hit the roof of the tunnel. I slid forward and repeated the caterpillar move again. This time the flashlight beam hit the biggest spider I had ever seen. It had a web blocking the tunnel and was only inches from my face. It moved at the beam of light, and I heard myself make some weird noise just before I blasted it with the .45 and tried to scoot backwards in utter, uncontrolled panic.

My right boot was being yanked away from me as the guys tried to pull me out of the tunnel. When they finally got me out, all I could do was lie on the ground hyperventilating. A couple of the guys had already pulled the pins on frags to throw into the hole. I stared up at a squad of Marines waiting for an explanation. The corpsman forced a canteen into my mouth, but drinking was impossible. When my mouth worked again, I realized my ears didn't. The ringing from firing a

.45 six times in the tunnel probably damaged my ears for life.

Eventually, the Lieutenant got me to speak. I started blabbering about a giant enemy spider. Their laughter was so hard and so loud it pierced even the church bells going off inside my ears.

* * * * *

As I was down in that trench tied to a backhoe, my mind was ten thousand miles away crawling through that spider hole with a .45. And that's when the trench caved in. If I had not been tied to that backhoe it would have been my last trench, and my last breath. I quit the job that day.

My second job was for the Downs Ford Funeral Home. I took it because at least I would be out of the sun, rain, and mud. They needed a security guard to stay at the place. They wanted someone to stay in a small apartment above the funeral home and be a night watchman. Military experience was a plus. It seemed perfect for me. With the martial arts and Marine Corps history, they loved me, so I was hired.

Soon I came to realize that guarding a funeral home is just a tad creepy. It got a whole lot creepier when I discovered that the job description included helping the mortician. Now, I had spent the night with dead Marines. I'd carried more than one dead friend onto a waiting medevac for the last ride. One of the times I was wounded, I was loaded into a chopper and placed among dead Marines. Believe me—that was unnerving.

So I had been around dead people, but working with a whistling mortician was just not a good thing for me at the time. One day they asked me if I could use my martial arts training to break a bone or two so we could make a fat dead guy fit into a coffin.

After that, I got a job at a Winn Dixie.

I started dating the sister of a high school buddy who had been killed in a car wreck. We foolishly got married. I was twenty and she was eighteen. She wasn't a Christian, and at the time I was saved, but no one except God would have guessed it by the way I was living. And listen, this book is not meant to be a confessional. If I wrote too much detail about what a sinful idiot I was, I'd probably be put in jail. Just know that there are not very many major sins that I have not committed. The only reason I write that is to let you know that God didn't give me all the answered prayers and a mind-blowing miracle on Graybeard Mountain because I was a choir boy. He did it because He loved me in spite of me. And if He can love a sinful clown like me, He can love you too. My hope is that readers will be as amazed at God's love and mercy as I am.

7

COLLEGE, DIVORCE & THE RED BIKINI

It was 1971, and I had started going to school at St. Petersburg Junior College. The attitude on campus was anti-war, and some of the so-called professors were stoking the fire with left-wing propaganda. Hearing their version of what was going on ten thousand miles away was very difficult for me. One day a professor started lecturing the class about Southeast Asia and, of course, it led to him running his liberal mouth about our criminal military. So I squared the clown away, and I thought he was going to faint. I was asked to leave the classroom.

There was another incident with a professor. I turned in an assignment, and this professor lost it. When I insisted that I turned it in he called me a liar in front of the class. I hit him in the face with another balled up homework assignment. I may have threatened to put him in a body bag or something to that effect. The college brought me in to see the dean. They were going to kick me out of college, but because I was attending on this disabled vet/GI Bill program, they changed their minds. It seemed very politically motivated, or maybe it was just economics, but they decided to let me stay when I promised that I would not attack any more professors.

I had a humanities professor who I really liked. He really liked me, too. He was a former FBI man, and he knew I was a Nam vet. We got along like friends, and I would even take him off campus to lunch because he loved riding in my 1949 Super Nash. I grew to respect him a lot. Quite often in class, he would lecture us on world creation stories. He constantly compared the Bible to all of the other creation stories. He loved to attack Christianity by trying to convince us that it was just like other religious myths: Hinduism, Buddhism, Islam, and on and on. One day he was going through his usual description of the Bible and comparing it to the Quran and the I-Ching.

A young girl raised her hand and was called on. She stood up and proceeded to give the prof a lesson on apologetics that I've never forgotten. After she showed him the stupidity of his comparisons and his total lack of knowledge of the Bible, my hero professor stood before the classroom no longer looking like a towering guru genius. Instead, he appeared an aging fool spouting nonsense to a bunch of trusting kids.

That young girl deserved all the medals I had stuffed in a seabag in my mom's attic. It took a few years for me to get my act together, but that girl made a difference in my life. I never forgot the courage it took for her to shoot down everyone's favorite professor in front of a hostile classroom of adoring students. If you're reading this and are in college or have kids in college, don't be naïve about what our university system has become. It may have started in the sixties and seventies, but it is far worse now.

But it would take more than that young girl's courage to bring me back to Christ. I was angry and bitter and probably a little dangerous. I started drinking pretty heavily, and drugs were the most popular thing going, so I joined in. A small fraternity asked me to pledge, and I did, but only after they waived all the pledging nonsense with a special exception for Nam vets.

Soon I started selling pot out of our small apartment. At one point, some drug dealers asked me to act as their security because I knew about guns and how to kill people. They were about to smuggle in cocaine from Mexico in a small plane. They wanted me to be their gunman, and, because I had made a couple of jumps, they wanted me to parachute out of the plane not far from a small air strip in Arizona with a backpack full of coke to be picked up by people on the ground. The money would be good.

I was so disillusioned with nearly everything that I just didn't care anymore. I wanted adventure, and the Marine Corps wouldn't let me re-up due to nerve damage in my leg. I said yes to the parachute deal. Would I have gone through with it? Probably not, but I can't be sure. Like I said, nothing mattered.

For reasons I never knew, the deal fell through, and I lost contact with those guys. A few months later, they must have tried it with another guy that I knew. He wasn't a Nam vet, but he was a martial artist. The plane crashed, and they were all killed. Of course, I know now that God kept me out of that plane for His purposes. I marvel at the Lord's mercy in my life.

I got a job at the post office and became a mailman. It was a good job, and the money was great. My wife was a legal secretary, and we bought a house. But I wasn't happy, and neither was she.

It was always a mistake for me to look at a newspaper or turn on the nightly news. The national media seemed as if they were all working for Hanoi. The left-wing propaganda was pounding our nation with half-truths and outright lies concerning Vietnam, and the American public was soaking it up.

I didn't fit in anymore and decided that I needed to get back into the Corps, so I tried to re-up again. I went to another state to re-up with different recruiters, but because the Corps was downsizing and I had the bullet wounds, they wouldn't take me. Meanwhile, my combat fatigue was getting more serious, and I struggled to sleep.

One morning I woke up to my wife's screams. At that moment, the sound seemed like incoming B-40 rockets, and I reached for my gun and KA-BAR. It took a few seconds to figure out what was happening, but soon I saw her pointing at my pillow. An awful lot of my hair had fallen out and covered the pillow. We both freaked out. I had no clue what was happening to me.

I went to the VA again.

"It looks like we misdiagnosed you, Mr. Clark," The VA doctor said as he studied me and my combat records as if I were some science project. "You do not have mild combat fatigue. I'm afraid that this is a sign of severe combat fatigue. I am going to up your dosage of Valium."

Most of my hair grew back, but I started to spiral down, farther and farther away from the Lord. I was drowning in a sea of drugs, booze, and anger. I was a terrible husband, so of course my marriage was a wreck. We were too young. Add to that a guy self-medicating his combat fatigue with drugs, and we had no chance. She wasn't a Christian and wanted nothing to do with church or the Bible, so we couldn't go to the Lord as a couple for help.

I always talked to God, even when I was acting like a total loser. I would ask God for help even though I knew I didn't deserve any help. In 1972 the Lord put a godly man named Joe beside me every morning as I got my mail ready to deliver. It was just what I needed, and I began to pray for forgiveness, wisdom, and direction. I really wanted to get my act together, especially with God. I even started having a few Christians from work over to my house to study the Bible. My wife was so against it that she would go in our bedroom, lock the door, and turn up the TV. Divorce was inevitable, and as is the case in most divorces, we were both to blame.

As I look back at my life, it's easy to see now that even during something as painful as a divorce, the Lord had His hand on me. God does not condone divorce, and I didn't want it, but it ended up being a blessing. More than once God removed people from my life who stood in the way of me coming back to Him. But divorce is like dealing with the death of someone you love.

Depression and bitterness consumed me after the divorce. One morning I woke up on St. Pete Beach still in my Post Office uniform, hungover, with a pistol in my hand. I lay there in the surf staring at the pistol for a long time. When I decided to stand, I noticed it was time to go work, so I went into the post office in that condition, soaking wet and hungover with a gun in my pocket.

About six months later, I put my house up for sale and decided to join the Rhodesian Army. They were in a war at the time and were paying $10,000 taxfree to former U.S. Marines with combat experience. It was not easy to enlist, but I managed to contact people at the Rhodesian embassy through *Soldier of Fortune* magazine. Because of my martial arts experience, they told me that I could make even more money by also becoming an instructor for hand-to-hand combat. I was all over that and told them I wanted to join.

I was working at the post office during the day and teaching Tae Kwon Do at night at the University of South Florida. There was a for-sale sign in my front yard, and I was in the process of getting my passport to go to Rhodesia when a friend named Terry and his girlfriend Val dropped by my house.

Terry was trying to hook me up with Val's best friend, Nancy Diez. Terry and Val had been telling me how beautiful she was and that she still lived at home with her parents, who were only about a block away. Val had stolen Nancy's driver's license from her purse to show me her photo.

"Are you kidding?" I asked with a laugh as I handed the license back to Val. "I thought you clowns said she was beautiful!" I glared at Terry to let him know that he was traitor to the male sex, and he started laughing.

"She is! I swear!" He shouted. "You can't go by a driver's license. You've probably even seen her! She lives right around the corner, middle of the block, big palm tree out front. She drives a little brown Toyota."

I paused with a delightful thought. I had just seen a smokin' hot babe in a bikini washing her car in a front yard on that very street. She was so hot that I didn't even see what kind of car it was. I doubted they were the same person, but I asked Val anyway. "Does she ever wash her car in the front yard in a red bikini?"

"I don't know, probably."

"Long black hair?"

"Yes."

"I'm in."

Val got on the phone and called Nancy. She told her we'd be there in a minute to pick her up to go to the old Beach Theater. I had never been on a blind date in my life. As we piled into Terry's car for the two-block drive to Nancy's house, I was a little nervous.

We pulled into the Diez driveway, and I got out, walked up to the door, rang the doorbell, and waited . . . and waited. I rang it again.

Suddenly the door yanked open, and I was face to face with a black-haired young woman who was pretty but had an angry scowl.

"Would you go away." She slammed the door in my face. I was immediately ticked off, and turned to look at the car for an explanation. Val leaned out of the passenger side window and yelled.

"Hurry up! The movie starts in ten minutes!"

I faced the door again and knocked instead of using the doorbell. The same girl opened the door and slammed it in my face again. Now I was ticked off. Val yelled from the car, "Knock again! That's her sister, Mary! That's not her."

I mumbled some Marine Corps terminology and knocked again and rang the doorbell. This time, a beautiful girl with long black hair opened the door.

"I'm so sorry! That was my sister. She can be a little weird."

I found out later that Nancy had broken up with a former boyfriend, and her fruitcake sister Mary wanted her to get back together with him. Her sister Mary is still a fruitcake, but I've grown to love her in spite of it over the years.

Nancy and I found free passes to the next movie in our popcorn that night, so we had an immediate second date. As most of the men reading this book will understand, Nancy Diez was so hot that my plans to join the Rhodesian Army were put on hold.

Soon, Nancy joined my Tae Kwon Do class at the University of South Florida. Then she started coming to private classes that I taught in my backyard Do Jang. One day she gave me a really cool long sleeved shirt with something embroidered on the breast pocket. It might have been my initials I can't remember for sure. She had made this shirt herself. She also made some of the dresses that she wore. Not very many girls in my life could make their own clothes. That shirt meant more to me than any shirt I'd ever worn. Nancy worked at Sears as a bookkeeper. She was really smart and incredibly squared away. Her parents didn't buy her a car. She worked and bought it herself and paid her own insurance. This beautiful knockout was the whole package. I could go on and on, but suffice it to say, we fell in love. I never made it to Rhodesia.

Our love for each other grew, but as much as I loved Nancy, I was afraid to marry her. After my first marriage had failed, it was clear to me that getting married to a girl who wanted nothing to do with God would be a fatal mistake. I never wanted to marry a girl who wasn't a Christian. I know that sounds ridiculous since I was living like anything but a Christian, but as messed up as I was, I had figured out one thing for sure. Marriage didn't have a chance if the two couldn't pray to Jesus Christ when things got tough. But it had to be Jesus we prayed to—nobody else.

Once when I was a kid in West Virginia, we visited a friend in a Catholic hospital. There was a big statue of Mary there that was worn away at the bottom and being replaced because people would bow down before that statue and kiss its feet. Mom told me that they had actually worn away the granite feet of this huge statue. As I watched this strange ritual, it gave me the creeps.

91

Even at eight or nine years old, something seemed wrong with kissing statues of Mary. When I asked Dad, he told me that many Catholics prayed to Mary. As I got older, I found out more about Catholic rituals, and when Nancy and I began to date, I had some serious conversations with her parents. I loved her mom and dad. We became very close before they died, but these conversations, especially with her mom, became more important as Nancy and I fell deeply in love. I did not want to marry anybody who prayed to Mary, and they did not want Nancy to marry anyone who was not Catholic.

Her mom told me that Mary was perfect and sinless, and that they prayed to Mary to ask her to entreat Jesus. She was like a middleman. I showed her mom *First Timothy, 2:5*, It says that *"For there is one God, and one mediator also between God and men, the man Christ Jesus."* I said that Mary couldn't be perfect and sinless because she was human. When I said Mary had other children after Jesus, Mrs. Diez went off and called that blasphemy. So I showed her that some of their names are actually given in scripture, and the Book of James was even written by the half-brother of Jesus.

I showed her *Acts 4:12*, which reads, *"And there is salvation in no one else; for there is no other name under heaven that has been given among men, by which we must be saved."* What was sad about all of these conversations was that this wonderful woman had been going to church religiously for her entire life and knew nothing about the Bible. Nancy's dad knew even less.

I thought this religion stuff might be a deal breaker, but I was willing to lose her over this. To my surprise, she already had her own questions about Catholicism that she wanted answered. She said she had never been taught what the Bible actually said. That was a big moment for both of us. We decided to find a Bible-teaching church.

As I've grown spiritually through the years, I see the false doctrine in the Catholic Church, *but* I can also see a lot of the good in the Catholic Church. No other church stands any stronger than they do against abortion. Many Catholics realize that you don't pray to anyone but Jesus Christ, and a lot of Catholics do not believe that the Pope speaks for God.

At the time when Nancy and I made this big life-changing decision, my Biblical education was better than hers, but not by much. My dad went to an old-time Pentecostal church, and as a kid I hated it. So my Mom took me to a Methodist church, and we kept going to the Methodist church even after we moved to St. Pete. It was good for me, but most of the sermons were topical with some verses sprinkled in. The truth is, I was probably at about a seventh-grade level in my understanding of what the Bible actually teaches.

Nancy and I played hit and miss as we searched for a church for a bit, and we both knew then and know now that there is no such thing as a perfect church, but we found one that felt right. We started going to a little church called Grace Bible Church. Grace Bible Church was life-changing for both of us. In one year we learned more about the Bible than we had learned in a combined forty years of going to the other churches. We started going to a Bible study at Pastor Engelman's house, and it was a time of growth that made a difference for the rest of our lives. Duffy Johnson was the assistant pastor, and many years later Duffy asked me to speak at his church in Vermont. That was the only time I have ever spoken publicly about the miracle on Graybeard Mountain.

8

THE WEAK LINK

I was still a letter carrier during the day and teaching Tae Kwon Do in the evening at USF. At the time, I was in very good shape. My resting heartrate was 38, and I was training to fight in the World Games. My grandmaster, Dong Keun Park, wanted me to compete so that I could qualify for the Olympics. Tae Kwon Do was a demo sport, not an official sport in the Olympics at the time, but Park was positive that it would be soon. He wanted me on the U.S. team. So I was flying to New York to train with him occasionally with that goal in mind.

GRANDMASTER DONG KEUN PARK

Master Dong Keun Park was not just another Korean master. I had begun martial arts in

Okinawa with Grandmaster Shimabuku in a style named Shorinryu. Shimabuku was a very special man, and I wanted to continue Shorinryu, but when I couldn't find any decent Shorinryu schools in my area, I was ready to give it up. That's when a good friend named Larry Miller came to the rescue.

Larry had trained with the great Dong Keun Park in Thailand while he was an Army linguist. The King of Thailand had requested through the President of Korea that Dong Keun Park be sent to Thailand to teach Tae Kwon Do. Park was a legend; he had fought in over 270 matches throughout Asia and had never been defeated. Even when various nations would insist on using the rules of their particular form of fighting to help their fighter win, they could not beat Park. He set many records, which I doubt anyone will ever break.

One night in New York, Master Park took me to a Korean nightclub. Two Korean bouncers stopped me at the door and wanted to know what I was doing here. Park told them I was his senior student, and they bowed, apologizing as they opened the doors. Inside I quickly discovered that I was the only non-Korean face in the very crowded nightclub. A famous female Korean singer was performing, and I guess it was a special night, but I don't know why.

During a break in the entertainment, a distinguished man in a very expensive suit came up to our table and began talking to me as if he knew me. He was extremely kind and told me how much he had heard about me. I thanked him, of course, having no clue who this guy was. When he left, I asked Master Park, "Who was that? He was a very a nice man."

"John, this same same, Kissinger."

I don't remember if Mr. Kissinger was the Secretary of State at the time but I found out what he meant. This nice man was the Korean Secretary of State.

When Dong Keun Park came to test my students and play golf, he stayed at my house. The phone would constantly ring with calls from Koreans, usually other masters. One day while he was staying at my house, the phone rang and I answered. The Korean man on the other end immediately asked me if this was Master Clark. I said yes, and he told me what a pleasure it was to talk to me and that he had heard such wonderful things about me. He was so gracious, and I naturally thought it was another Korean master. I asked him if he would like to speak to Master Park, and he said yes.

I got Master Park, and he spoke with the man for a few minutes and finally hung up. I was really curious about the call and curious about who this guy was and how he knew me.

"Sahbumnim," I said when he hung up the phone. "Who was that master? He seemed to know me, and he was a very gracious man."

"John!" His face was stern. "This President Park."

It was the President of Korea calling to talk to Master Dong Keun Park on my phone. I'm pretty sure I must be on every FBI list we have after that phone call. All that being said, I'm sure you can understand that being the senior student of this man was very special to me, and training with him to fight in the World Games was no small event.

But the Lord had different plans, and once again, Nam played a role. My body had a weak link thanks to the Vietnam War.

* * * * *

In June, 1968, Alpha Company, First Battalion, Fifth Marines had finally been brought back to Phu Bai for a day of rest and a hot meal. We never bathed except for being in the rain or walking across rivers and our utilities, clothes, were torn or ripped up by the jungle. The luxury of being able to sleep on a cot instead of the ground and out of the rain was no small thing to grunts who had been in the bush for extended periods of time.

Phu Bai meant a real meal, a chance to actually take a shower with real soap, and new clothes. It also meant a drink at the Animal Pit. As much as I wanted a shower, I wanted a beer even more. You almost forget what things like beer or Coke taste like. So Chan and I dropped our packs inside the Second Platoon tent and headed for The Animal Pit.

It was an Army bar/bunker covered with sandbags. An Army MP stood out front collecting weapons but not pistols or KA-BARs. I dropped off my M60, Chan handed the MP his M-16, and in we went.

It was like entering another world— a strange cross between an old west saloon and some futuristic bar where the men were armed and dangerous. There was a juke box blaring "Sitting on The Dock of the Bay." It was a mixture of troops: some Army Green Berets sat at one table, Korean Marines at another, and there were some 101st Airborne soldiers.

It was easy to spot the Marines. We wore faded jungle fatigues/utilities, we were unshaven, and man we stunk. Of course, we couldn't smell ourselves anymore, but we knew how bad we smelled by the way the other troops sat as far away from us as possible.

The walls were made of plywood and decorated with black-and-white photos of Army generals and a couple of shot-up red and blue NVA flags with the yellow star. There were some captured enemy weapons hanging behind the bar, a couple of AK-47's and a couple of B-40 rocket launchers.

Chan spotted Gunny McDermott, Corporal Swift Eagle, and another Marine named, Sam at a table near a pinball machine, so we sat with them. These were hard-core Marines, and I really admired them.

The Gunny was an old man, probably around thirty-five. He had seen it all and seemed to be absolutely fearless. He had a half-dozen Purple

Hearts and a Silver Star and I wasn't sure what else. Then there was this crazy Native American. I was really glad he was on our side. About seven months later, I ran across an open field under fire with Corporal Swift Eagle and saw him earn his seventh Purple Heart.

I could have sat there for hours just listening to these guys, but I only had about twenty minutes. Chan brought us our second can of Schlitz from the bar just as Corporal Bob Carrol came through the front door in full combat gear with his radio on his back.

"Second Platoon! Alpha-One-Five! Saddle up! Choppers waiting! We gotta' rescue 'Special Forces' again!"

There were many four-letter words bellowed in response, but Bob just turned and headed off. We hustled back to the big tent for our gear, and I really regretted not getting to take that shower or eat that hot meal.

We formed up for a double-time jog to a waiting Chinook. Chan and I went up the ramp first because the lieutenant wanted the gun team off-loading last so they could form a perimeter and point the machine gun team to where the most fire was needed if we landed in a hot landing zone.

Not long after we lifted off, the co-pilot turned and yelled, "We're flying into a hot LZ!"

Flying into a hot landing zone meant we'd be about as helpless as we could be. At eighteen-years-old, it was also about as exciting as anything life could offer. Twenty minutes later, we circled over a couple of mountains and then seemed to pick up speed as we dropped into a valley. It was like that feeling you get in a roller-coaster when it does the plunge.

"Lock and load, Marines!" the lieutenant bellowed, and all the men started chambering rounds and flipping off the safeties. I had a fifty-round short belt in the M60 and pulled back the bolt to chamber the first round.

The Chinook had little port-hole windows so we could see below as the chopper tilted. I got a look at a couple of rice paddies and could see tracer fire coming up out of the surrounding jungle. The Chinook slowed drastically, the back end with the ramp settled, and somebody screamed.

"Move out!"

We were taking a lot of fire, and bullets started smacking through the tin hull of that chopper. On those occasions the pilot and co-pilot don't completely land: they hover with the front wheels off the ground and the ramp barely touching so they can drop off the Marines and take off fast.

Chan and I were filing toward the ramp and Chan made it off, but just as I reached the ramp, the chopper swung violently to one side, and I was thrown against the hull. I glanced toward the front of the Chinook and saw that the pilot had been killed and was slumped between the seats. The chopper started going in circles just off the ground, and I was tossed around like a pinball.

The co-pilot gained control and lifted off, but I was on my back with a hundred pounds of gear strapped to me. By the time I scrambled to my feet to make a run for the ramp, we were probably forty feet off the ground. It was a split-second decision whether to risk the jump or stay on board. I blindly jumped and probably should have died.

I was eighteen years old and very strong. But I had a twenty-five pound machine gun, four hundred rounds of heavy ammo, numerous grenades, a cartridge belt, two canteens, a KA-BAR, a .45 caliber pistol and clips, an entrenching tool, a flak-jacket, a helmet, and a heavy pack. I landed like an anchor, but God dumped me in a rice paddy. I was alive, but my back would never be the same, it would always be a weak link. All of the training in the Marine Corps, and martial arts after the Corps kept me strong enough to avoid surgery until one fateful morning in 1973.

* * * * *

One day on my mail route while delivering heavy boxes of books to Haslam's Book Store, my back popped. That was it. The weak link gave way. The damaged back had finally fully herniated, and my hope of fighting in the World Games or the Olympics was gone.

While lying in a hospital bed in traction and trying very hard to avoid surgery, I had lots of time to think about my next move. The opportunity I'd had for teaching an accredited course in martial arts at the University of South Florida was now history. I had planned to quit the post office as soon as the university made my class an accredited course, but suddenly both jobs were gone. Nancy worked at Sears, and her paychecks fed us. But we were pretty broke.

9

GUNS UP!

In 1975 my frustration with the media's liberal slant on the Vietnam War had not lessened one bit. Hollywood's version of Vietnam was all that American kids were seeing. The nightly news made me want to shoot my television set. In 1973, after just twelve days of B-52 strikes on North Vietnam, the communists gave up and came to the Paris Peace Talks.

The war ended on our terms, and the American military pulled out of Vietnam. We forced them to give up the fight. Where I come from, that's called a win. After all American combat troops were gone, the North Vietnamese broke the treaty and invaded the South. The war went on for nearly three more years before the South surrendered.

Every Nam vet I knew was deeply angered by that, but we were even angrier about the slant the media was putting on it. The U.S. military was being blamed for having lost the war even though American combat troops hadn't been in Vietnam for three years. Arguing about it made me want to hit people.

One day a friend told me that I needed to write a book and tell what the Marines really did in Nam. I started giving that a lot of thought and talked to Nancy about it. She told me that she thought it was a great idea. She suggested that I start taking some creative writing courses at St. Pete College.

That was it: the quest began. If we ever had kids, at least they would have a record of what their dad did in Nam and wouldn't have to rely on some idiot in Hollywood or the liars on TV news. We didn't own a typewriter, so I just used a pencil and soon I had nearly two hundred pages written.

I signed up for a non-credit creative writing course at the college. It was being taught by a guy named Fred Wright, who had over six-hundred stories and articles published and had been a journalist. He teamed up with a woman named Marvette Carter, and they would take up to ten pages a week from each student, critique it, and help you with every facet of writing. The most important thing Fred taught me was to write like you talk. Since I was a D- student in high school and college English, writing like I talk was the only way I knew how to write.

Each week Fred and Marvette seemed to be very impressed with my story but not impressed with my handwriting. One week Fred told me that this story had a chance to get published, but I would have to get a typewriter. I had taken typing in high school just so I could get an easy grade to stay on the football team. Little did I know what a blessing that would become in my life.

Nancy and I were broke, so buying a typewriter wasn't going to happen. I was still getting large bottles of medications mailed to me from the VA, Darvon for pain and Valium for combat fatigue. I had a high school football buddy who was now a druggie. His name was Steve Kersker, and he was always looking for pills or pot.

I honestly don't remember how I found out that Steve had a typewriter, but he did. There were zero dollars in our budget to buy it, so Steve traded it to me for a couple of bottles of pills.

Yeah, I know I was not exactly a poster boy for Christian ethics, but believe me, if this was the worst of my sins, I'd be wearing wings.

In spite of the sin in my life, the Lord heard my prayers for help. He forgave me and allowed me to experience a series of miracles. Though nothing was as dramatic as the one on Graybeard Mountain, each was wonderful and humbling. Our God's love for us is off the chart, but we can only experience it if we are not too prideful to seek Him. I kept talking to the Lord through war and depression. I had to. I don't think I could have gone through a day without talking to God. There's a verse that encourages me about that very thing. There's a verse that made me feel like it was okay with God if I griped and complained to Him sometimes. *Psalm 55:* 16-17 encourages me in that habit. It reads, *"As for me, I shall call upon God, And the Lord will save me. Evening and morning and at noon, I will complain and murmur, and He will hear my voice."* Brother, that's me. I complain and murmur and thank Him constantly.

By the way, years later I had the privilege of leading that druggie, Steve Kersker, to Christ. I certainly was not always a great example for Steve, but he trusted me and started going to church with Nancy and me. His life changed dramatically. Steve went home to be with the Lord a few years ago, and I know we will see each other again.

The writing class was about ten weeks long, then off a couple of weeks, and then they'd start up a new one. I took that class about fifteen times. I finally got my entire book critiqued, and it ended up being around four hundred pages. Fred and Marvette were convinced that my book was one of the best war books they'd ever read. Of course that was great to hear from two pros, but I never really thought it would actually get published.

I started submitting the manuscript to every publisher I could find and started submitting excerpts from the book to every magazine that would take submissions.

When my son Shawn was born, my office became a bedroom. So I tore a hole in the roof of our house over the dining room and built a small six-by-eight foot office that looked more like a conning tower for a submarine. There was a small telephone pole just outside my backyard fence that was no longer used. With the help of a neighbor, I cut it down with a chainsaw, and we fashioned a unique spiral staircase into my conning tower. As you can imagine, Nancy and my neighbors were thrilled with this new addition to our home.

The office didn't seem to matter, though. After four years of trying to sell the book and everything else I had written, my successes amounted to exactly zero. Fred told me to do something creative with all of the rejections to keep up my spirits. So by early 1984, I had wallpapered my entire office with rejections on top of rejections.

My back was healed up, but any shot at the World Games or Olympics was gone. I ran a Do Jang out of my backyard to make some extra money and was working at an electronics business in Tampa. Nancy and I were still going to a Bible study at Pastor Phil Engelman's house. In spite of being low on money, it was a wonderful time of spiritual growth in our lives. The Bible study was a great chance to pray for others too.

It was like most Bible studies. We were a group of Christians or people searching for the truth who all had their own problems and needs. We would have small homework assignments like memorizing a scripture verse. At the end of each

Thursday night study, we'd pray for various needs in the group and for our nation. There were people out of work and marriages in trouble and concerns for our children and sicknesses.

Early on in the Thursday night studies, when it came time to toss in a prayer request, I asked for prayer for my book to get published. Of course I told them I'd been getting rejections for nearly four years but had not totally given up yet. That was it. Now every single Thursday the group would pray for Johnnie's book to get published. No one in the group had ever read the book.

My guilt got heavier and heavier each Thursday until I wanted to crawl under the carpet when someone would pray for Johnnie's book to get published. The reason is this. I wrote *Guns Up!* out of anger and wanted the book to tell the truth about what the Marines did in Vietnam. There seemed to be no way to make it real without the dialogue being real.

Well, in case you've never been around combat Marines, they cuss. *Guns Up!* couldn't have been written without profanity. But one of the reasons I wrote the book was so that my children would know that their dad and hundreds of thousands of other guys like their dad were not over there killing women and children like colleges and the media and Hollywood wanted them to think.

Now, as I became a stronger Christian, the thought of my kids reading a book with a bunch of four-letter words really concerned me. One Thursday night we got a new verse to memorize, and for whatever reason, this verse would not let me go. It was I Samuel 2:30 and one part of the verse reads *"I did indeed say that your house and the house of your father should walk before Me forever"*; but now the Lord declares, *'Far be it from Me— for those who honor me I will honor . . .'*

I am hardly the first Christian who has been haunted by a verse, but God drove me nuts with this verse. You have to realize that I had written and rewritten *Guns Up!* over many years. It was not a real happy endeavor, even though I wanted to be a writer. It was like going through Nam again and again for me. Guys I loved were getting killed over and over in my head. To me, their sacrifices were being spit on by an ungrateful nation. My VA counselors thought writing about Nam would be cathartic. It was not. The idea of rewriting that book again made me nauseous. I refused to even contemplate it.

But each Thursday night, the people in the Bible study would pray for Johnnie's book to get published. And each Thursday night, we'd do our memory verses, and up would pop that verse, *"For those who honor Me I will honor."* I honestly reached a point where I didn't want their prayers anymore.

Guns Up! had a Christian story in it because of my A-gunner Richard Chan. And the truth is, I've never been shy about witnessing for Christ and did so in Vietnam. I wanted very much for the book to be a witness for Jesus Christ because that had always been the most important part of this exciting and, evidently, very touching story of some incredibly brave men.

I finally took the book to my pastor and asked him to read it. I told him that God was really hounding me with that stupid verse but there was no way this story could be rewritten. It would be easier to go to the dentist every day for a year than rewrite this "fricken" book.

Phil was blown away by the book, but he was no help. He told me a decision like that had to be between me and the Lord. I talked it over with

Nancy and decided to call my old professors, Fred and Marvette. I told them I was going to do a rewrite on the book and why. Fred and Marvette are not Christians, so the reason for rewriting the book seemed ridiculous or at least unnecessary to them. I had once asked them if they were Christians, and Fred said with all seriousness, "Well, I suppose we are, since we live in America."

They were both against removing the cursing and told me that they thought *Guns Up!* was the best war novel they had ever read. They told me no one would believe a Vietnam War book as remotely realistic without the language. "It will sound like Howdy Doody joins the Marine Corps!"

These were the two people I trusted most when it came to writing. Hearing their praise for the book, and hearing their warning about taking out the curse words, had an impact on me. God used these two people to get that book written. I had agonized over that stupid book, and it had been rejected by every publisher from New York to California for four years. The truth was, I didn't really believe it would ever actually get published, with or without curse words.

Another Thursday night came, and so did the prayer request and petitions to the Lord. I started feeling like I had an anchor around my neck. I prayed about it that night—a lot. The next morning I started the rewrite. It took months for me to rewrite and retype the entire manuscript. The day I finished that job, I drank some champagne and felt a hundred pounds lighter.

Six days after finishing the revision, I got a phone call from *American Legion Magazine*. The editor told me they wanted to buy a story that I had sent them. I was dumbfounded and told the guy that I never sent them a story. He said, "Well, I have it right here. It's titled 'The Battle for Truoi Bridge' by Johnnie Clark. An excerpt from a book titled, *Guns Up!*"

For a couple of moments, I was speechless as I tried to remember sending *American Legion* magazine a story. "When did I send you that story?"

"Let's see here . . . yes here it is . . . oh, you sent it to us in 1980."

"Four years ago! And you're just now finding it?"

"It's been in our slush pile, I guess. Anyway, one of our editors found it, and we're very excited about it. We'll pay you $300.00 for it."

I was blown completely away. Of course I said yes and rushed to tell Nancy. We celebrated. It was the first thing I'd ever sold after years of writing. I hadn't gotten down the first glass of champagne when the phone rang again. Nancy overheard the conversation, and we were both shocked. It was a call from *Soldier of Fortune* magazine. They wanted to publish one of my stories from *Guns Up!* It had turned up in their slush pile and was dated four years earlier, but for reasons they could not explain, it had just now been discovered.

Then *Eagle Magazine* out of New York called, and it was the same ridiculous conversation. When the last magazine called me, all within one week of the rewrite, I sort of figured out that this was a God thing. There were no cuss words in those magazine stories. I'm not sure why I removed them before submitting the stories, but I think it was probably because of some standard guidelines list that Fred handed out in class for magazine submissions.

I immediately started sending out the book again. Now, there was a rule back then put out by publishers about multiple submissions. They would not accept a book that had been mailed to other publishers. What a joke for writers. The writer was supposed to sit and wait for at least three months—during which time they'd probably get a rejection from a publisher—before sending it to another publisher. At that rate, a writer could be two hundred years old before he ever got published. I ignored that rule and sent *Guns Up!* to multiple publishers.

Within one month, nine book publishers suddenly wanted *Guns Up!* I was in my conning tower trying to write a new book, *The Harlot's Cup,* when the phone rang. It was a lady named Pamela Strickler from Random House and Ballantine Books. She wanted to publish *Guns Up!*

I immediately recognized that name. I asked her to hold on for a moment as I searched my walls of rejections. There it was! The personally signed rejection letter from Pamela Strickler of Random House/Ballantine Books.

"Miss Strickler, why do you want the book now?"

"Now?"

"Yes. You rejected this book about a year ago. And I'm an expert on rejection letters, so you

119

actually had to have read at least part of the book." I proceeded to read the letter to her then I said, "And you signed this—it's not a stamp of your name like many are."

"If I wrote that, I definitely read the book. I do not tell authors that I read a book if I didn't."

"So why do you want it now? It's the same book you rejected, except I took out the cuss words."

"What? Are you saying there is no profanity in this book?"

"Not a word of it."

"Well, Mr. Clark, I'm quite shocked. Every reader and junior editor has read this book at Ballantine. I'm the senior editor, and I just read the book, and not one reader or editor noticed that there are no curse words."

"My war sure didn't change."

"I've never seen a Vietnam War story without profanity. I'm quite sure that when we have the final editorial meeting, our editors will want you to put some of the language back into the manuscript. Just for realism, you understand."

I don't think I spoke for a couple of seconds while I marveled at this conversation and the incredible temptations Satan could use to screw a man up. This was the number one publisher in the world, and up to the last month, I'd gone years without getting a single word published anywhere. But even Johnnie Clark wasn't stupid enough to fall for this bait. I knew a miracle when it slapped me in the face consistently for a month.

I had chosen to honor God in this simple part of my life. Look, I know to some people it probably seems almost childish to make such a big deal out of a few four-letter words. But the Lord knew my heart, and He knew my struggle, and He knew that I really wanted to honor Him in this.

I finally laughed. "Miss Strickler, there are two chances I'll put the cuss words back into that manuscript, slim and none, and slim just left town."

They published the book. It made a couple of bestseller lists at one time, and it is now in a thirty-fifth printing or something like that. Matter of fact, it just got published in Lithuania! I have a father and his two sons in my Do Jang from Lithuania. They've trained with me for years. They go back to visit family there. They bought a few copies of *Guns Up!* while they were there. It is really   cool.

The title is spelled like this: KULKOSVAIDZIUS PARUOST!

I'm adding this as a side note because I just received a letter from a young Lithuanian soldier with a copy of the book. He asked me to sign it, and in his letter, he told me that he believes this is the greatest war book God ever created. He told me that his mates were all reading it, and it was a great witness for Jesus Christ. It just gives me chill bumps each time an email or letter like this comes to me.

Ballantine Books asked me to write another book, so I did. It's titled *Semper Fidelis,* and both it and *Guns Up!* were on the commandant's list of suggested reading for all Marines.

After that, I wrote a series based on my gunny and another old Gunnery Sergeant from the Korean War named Francis Hugh Killeen. Their stories and adventures in the Corps were the kind of thing every American should hear about.

Since that simple decision to honor God, He has kept his promise to honor those who honor Him. My life has been filled with honors of all kinds, and I just giggle with joy every time I get another one, not because being honored is so important to me, but because I know why I'm receiving it.

God bestowing honors on me became an ongoing theme throughout my life. I was a kid who honestly did not know a noun from a verb, and to be perfectly honest, I'm still not sure half the time. In spite of being a terrible English student and least likely to ever be a writer, the Lord gave me a bestseller and eight other books. I've also been asked to speak in place of congressmen during Memorial Day celebrations. I've spoken on television and on ABC radio shows to over a million listeners. I've even spoken in churches on Sunday mornings. The honors and answered prayers that God has bestowed on me, both big and small, would take another book to compile.

I'm telling this story to encourage every Christian or person seeking to know Jesus Christ that He knows your heart, and He knows we are all sinners and pretty screwed up. For His own reasons, He loves us in spite of ourselves. He knows if you're sincere, it's not like you can fool God, and He honors those who honor Him. How he chooses to honor you is up to Him. He keeps his promises, but yeah, there's a catch. You can read about it in Matthew 6:33: *"But seek first His kingdom and His righteousness; and all these things shall be added to you."*

We have to have the proper goal, and then the by-product comes. *"Seek first His kingdom . . . and these things shall be added."* Proverbs 3:6 puts it this way: *"In all your ways acknowledge Him, and He will make your paths straight.*

And then there's *Joshua 1:8: "You shall meditate on it [God's word] day and night, so that you may be careful to do . . . then, you will make your way prosperous, and then you will have success."*

I'll be as honest as I can about these promises with no false humility. I think I have had the proper goals sometimes, but sometimes it seemed by pure accident. Of course the Holy Spirit was leading me, but I wasn't always aware of it. The truth is, I do sort of acknowledge God in most of my ways, and I do meditate day and night on the word, especially when I'm troubled.

For instance, I memorized the first part of *Psalm 37* just to stop my mind from worrying about crap at night. *"Do not fret . . . "* I fret myself. When I worry about this or that, I say this verse or others, and I remind God of some promise He made in scripture, and I then turn it over to the

Lord. *Psalm 37:4* reads, *"Delight yourself in the Lord; and He will give you the desires of your heart."* Sometimes I do delight myself in the Lord. Not always, but sometimes. So did I complete some prior condition, and was that why God gave me so many blessings and a jaw-dropping miracle on Graybeard Mountain? I don't know. God doesn't have to explain. He said in Romans, *"I will have mercy upon whom I will have mercy."*

I do know this much, though. When I went to that mountain, I was truly seeking to be alone with Him. I wasn't seeking the applause of men or trying to look holy to anyone. It was personal—just between me and Him.

10

CINCINNATI ENQUIRER

My Tae Kwon Do/Judo school continued to grow, and life settled into a normal pattern for each of us. I wrote in the morning, taught martial arts at night, and helped to raise our two kids, Shawn and Bonnie, all the time.

My wife, Nancy, has the work ethic of a coal miner, and if I didn't make enough money to pay our way, then she did. We had a Bible study in our home, mostly students and friends from my Do Jang. Some great things came out of that little Bible study. I like to think a few people even came to Christ.

Grandmaster Park became the head coach for the USA Olympic Team in Barcelona. All but one of the fighters medaled, and it was probably the most successful team we had in the Olympics.

I helped teach Grandmaster Park's son, John Park. Like most kids, he preferred to train with me than his dad because his dad was too mean. John grew up and runs his dad's school now, though the old Master overlooks it, of course. John and I tested in Korea together recently, and thanks to John, I was invited to teach hand-to-hand combat seminars at Annapolis and West Point—an incredible honor. The Parks consider me family, and I feel the same way about them.

Through the years, the Parks would send some of their students to Florida to train with me. According to some of the kids who come to train, there's a standing joke in the New York Do Jang. "If you want to win a Gold Medal, you train with Park. If you want to learn how to kill someone, you train with Clark."

As small groups of Park students came to train, I made a deal with them. The deal for these students coming to Florida was this. You stay with us, you go to the Bible study. It was not a request, but those kids were always very respectful, and, usually to their surprise, they loved it. I believe some may have found Christ.

* * * * *

One day in the late nineties, I got a packet in the mail. Inside, I found a number of folded newspaper articles from the *Cincinnati Enquirer*. A total stranger had sent them to me and asked me to read them to see if I recognized the Vietnam Marine that all these stories were about. The articles were letters sent home from Vietnam by a Marine named Richard Weaver. I didn't recognize his name, but the moment I read the first paragraph of the first letter home, I knew. It was Big Red. Someone thought these letters sounded just like a book they had read titled *Guns Up!*.

Reading those letters from Big Red was not easy. It is even difficult to write about right now, years later. He was a real hero, and like so many of the heroes I saw and served with, his sacrifice seemed for nothing. Getting these articles in the mail pushed me toward anger and frustration again. I guess I was a little depressed and probably more sad than angry. I loved Big Red.

Two high school friends of Big Red, Lon Deckard and Bill Wiedemann, had discovered what a great Marine their friend was, thanks, in part, to my book. Lon was a Nam vet, and Bill was an Army vet. They went to work like warriors to honor their friend. It was very inspiring.

It took thirty years and the help of an Ohio Congressman, but the Corps finally realized that Big Red, Richard Weaver, was a hero. They awarded Red a Bronze Star with combat V posthumously, and the city had a parade in his honor. It should have been The Navy Cross, but that's another story. A lot of the guys from the outfit came to honor Red, and it turned into a reunion.

The *Cincinnati Enquirer* did a big story with photos of me and Chan at the memorial. Because of the books, I was asked to speak a couple of times. When I spoke at Red's high school in Indian Hills, the response from the school and the guys from Alpha Company who were there was overwhelming. They unveiled a small monument with Red's medals in front of the school. It was very emotional for all of us.

That night in a hotel we had a few beers and way too many memories. The guys started talking about the night Cpl. Frank Burris was killed and what happened the next day. Frank was Sgt. Stacey Watson's best friend. They were both short-timers when Frank died, due to go home soon. We could have saved Frank that night, but we didn't find a second bullet wound, and he didn't tell us he had one. Stacey had never gotten over Frank's death. We couldn't get a medevac that night.

Frank Burris had a red-haired baby that he'd never seen, and he carried a photo of her in his helmet liner. We called her Red Baby Girl, and she was all he talked about. Getting home to see her was the only thing that mattered to Frank.

I wrote about the night Cpl. Frank Burris died in *Guns Up!* Thirty-one years after he died, Red Baby Girl read a book titled *Guns Up!* Though I didn't use Frank's real name, somehow she knew it was her dad. She found my address and sent me a larger version of that same baby photo that Frank carried in his helmet liner. I spent a few hours crying. She asked me to call her and tell her if that was her dad in *Guns Up!*. The conversation was very hard on me. I mentally went back to Nam for a few weeks or more. She had never seen her dad and was consumed by his memory and how he died.

Sgt. Stacey Watson was still bitter about losing Frank that night in Nam. It scarred him for the rest of his life. Stacey died a couple of years ago. That evening in Cincinnati, Stacey asked me if I remembered what happened the day after we put Frank's body on a chopper. I wasn't sure. Then he pulled out a photo album.

He had the photo I.D. of an NVA nurse we'd killed. I was in absolute shock. It was one of those memories of war that haunted me, and now I was looking at her photo. It had been a mercy killing to put her out of her misery: her wounds were horrific, and I had written about that day in the book, but I never dreamed I'd actually be looking at her photo and all of her personal information—I could even see where she was born. The guys seemed to remember that it was me who shot her because I had a .45.

Maybe that night in the hotel was filled with too many memories. Whatever the reasons, that couple of days in Cincinnati sort of sent me over the edge I'd been teetering on for a long time.

I went back home, but my mind went back to Nam. I was on an ambush every night, and sleep was nearly impossible. I drank a lot and got pretty mean in the Do Jang. I'm sure I lost the respect of more than one of my students, but one kid stands out.

I was in my office at our new Do Jang while one of my blackbelt instructors was teaching a class. My mind was on that NVA woman I killed right after Frank died. My instructor came in and told me he was dealing with a real jerk in the class who had been disrespectful in the past.

I came out and confronted the guy. One of my teenage blackbelts, a kid named Mike, was in that class. I blanked out in a rage. Mike's father told me it scared Mike, and soon after that, Mike quit the school. He was very disappointed in me. I really wanted to tell people that I was reliving some tough memories and that I was sorry for being a jackass, but it was too hard for me to explain.

I was constantly dwelling on Nam and all of the mistakes I'd made. There just seemed to be so many regrets. I found myself constantly wishing I could have done more. I wondered if things would have been different if I'd just been older. If I'd been twenty or twenty-one years old, I wouldn't have made eighteen-year-old mistakes. I prayed about it all of the time, but I just couldn't forgive myself for some of my failures.

It was around that time that I was contacted by an old Marine buddy named Pat McCrary, who lived near Jacksonville. He sent me a newspaper article. It was a story about him trying to get a Purple Heart license tag. They told him there was no proof of him ever being wounded. He showed them a bullet hole and angrily explained to them that this big scar wasn't from a bad dream, but they wouldn't budge. I remembered the event, of course. It happened in a graveyard in Vietnam. That night and that graveyard would play an important part in my life. I was with Pat that night in the Arizona Territory in An Hoa Valley.

* * * * *

It was late July, 1968, and Alpha Company was sweeping through a place we called Dodge City in the Arizona Territory a few miles outside of An Hoa Combat Base, twenty-five miles southwest of Da Nang. We had a kid with us named Umdemstock, who was from a ranch in Oklahoma, so we called him Cowboy. I grew to really care about this kid. I call him kid when he was probably a year older than me. His story is sad and inspiring and, to this day, a mystery. The mystery is how he got through Marine training.

133

I promise you, in 1967, Parris Island was not for the faint-hearted. I witnessed my drill instructors push a soft, overweight recruit until he had a hernia. This poor guy couldn't hack it physically or emotionally. The DIs screamed that they were going to drive him out of their Marine Corps because he was going to get Marines killed in Nam. And they drove him out of their Marine Corps.

I watched them push one recruit, who they saw as a weak link, to the point of climbing a two-hundred-foot water tower, where he then threatened to jump if they didn't let him off Parris Island. The senior drill instructor ordered an entire company of Marine recruits to form up around that water tower, then screamed that if he didn't jump, they would beat him out of the Corps when he came down. He came down, and they beat the crap out of him.

When we marched in close order drill on Parris Island, every Marine had to have his eyes glued to the back of the head of the Marine in front of him. One day as we marched in close order drill I glanced ever so slightly to my right. A Drill Instructor kicked me in the shin so hard it took me off my feet. The bruise lasted for a month. On another occasion, I decided to try to read a letter from home under a blanket at night with a flashlight. I found myself on the deck with the bunk bed on top of me. The next morning my three DI's put my right thumb in the chamber of an M14 rifle, slammed the bolt forward and pulled the trigger, sending the firing pin through my thumbnail. I was then ordered to stand at attention with my right arm out and the 9-pound rifle hanging from my thumbnail while I sang the Marines Hymn. Then I was ordered to recite the manual of arms.

Sometimes, they kicked or punched the guy who murdered a Marine Corps sand flea. Sometimes, they made him dig a six-by-six-foot grave for the sand flea.

Yeah, it sounds insane because it was insane, but the Corps was building professional killers who didn't slap mosquitoes or cough or tremble on ambushes. I hope to God they still train Marines that way, but for the sake of diversity and this PC culture, I fear they don't.

My point is this. Soft bodies and weaklings were weeded out of my Marine Corps to keep other Marines from dying in combat because of them.

That is why none of us could figure out how Cowboy made it through the gauntlet. He was the most terrified Marine any of us had ever met. He would get so scared that he would shake uncontrollably. Ambushes and three-man killer teams were not for the weak—believe me, it was stressful on the toughest Marines alive—but this kid would urinate all over himself. Sometimes his teeth would actually chatter so loudly that I thought he would get us all killed.

One day the lieutenant came to me and Chan. He told us he was putting Cowboy in our gun team. I don't know why or how—we all have different make-ups—but Chan and I managed to laugh a lot in Vietnam, and the LT thought we might be able to help the kid loosen up. He hoped that being with us might help him to stop being so nervous.

I knew the only thing that could help Cowboy was God. I think I felt sort of an urgency to talk to him about my faith. Chan and I started trying to show him some Bible verses. After a couple of weeks, we got to know him, and his story was pretty sad. I'm not going to write it because it could hurt some people in his family.

There is power in the word of God. That isn't just some Christian cliché: it is fact. I have seen scripture change a man's life. I watched this poor kid find some hope when he heard and read a couple of wonderful verses. I can't swear to it, but I believe these verses from Psalm 27 were some of the verses we had him read, and it seemed to help.

"The Lord is my light and my salvation;
Whom shall I fear?
The Lord is the defense of my life;
Whom shall I dread?
When evildoers came upon me to devour my flesh,
My adversaries and my enemies, they stumbled and fell.
Though a host encamp against me,
My heart will not fear;
Though war arise against me,
In spite of this I shall be confident....
Do not abandon me nor forsake me,
O God of my salvation!
For my father and my mother have forsaken me,
But the Lord will take me up."

Cowboy was only with our gun team a short while, but we saw him starting to rely on the Lord a little more. In spite of the hopeful signs, he was still way too nervous to be in combat with Marines, and we all knew it.

One morning as we sat in the mud, wet and miserable after an all-night ambush, the lieutenant walked toward our gun team with a concerned expression. He tried to put on a positive face as he dropped to a knee with his M-16.

"Cowboy, we got a chopper coming in with some C-rats and ammo, and you're getting on it. This is your ride home, Marine. I'm shipping you out of the bush. You're going back to the world."

Understand that at this point in that war, many men would have jumped at a chance to go back to the world and away from this nightmare. But especially someone fighting the inner terror that this kid was fighting. Somehow, with courage far beyond mine, this young Marine said no.

He was trembling, and his voice was shaky, but he was incredibly determined, maybe even a little angry as he said, "No! No, sir. I'm not going home until all the other Marines go home."

I am crying as I write this very vivid memory. Yes, I still cry every time I think or talk about this moment in my war. This terrified young boy was the bravest Marine I ever knew among an awful lot of heroic men. The lieutenant was as impressed with his courage as we were, and he agreed to let him stick it out a little longer.

We took some casualties right after that. Another gunner went down, and Chan had to take over the other machine gun. Cowboy was put back in a squad, and I got another A-gunner. A few days later we made contact during a sweep.

It was August 3, 1968. We were the lead platoon on a company-size sweep and had spotted three NVA soldiers near a tree line. We opened fire, hitting one of them. The other two dragged the wounded NVA into the tree line. We advanced through the tree line and found ourselves standing at the edge of an open graveyard about seventy-five meters across.

On the other side of the graveyard was a hootch, a wood and grass hut. Behind the hootch was a thick jungle area. We saw the two NVA dragging the wounded one into tree cover just to the right of that hootch. I was ordered to go forward and recon the other side with fire, so I went into the graveyard, stood on one of the round grave mounds, and opened fire, spraying the other side with about fifty or a hundred rounds. There was no return fire, so the captain ordered a squad across.

Pat McCrary and Cowboy were in that squad. Halfway across, an enemy battalion opened fire: three 30-caliber machine guns in fixed positions and way too many AK-47s to estimate raked the graveyard with thousands of green tracers. B-40 rockets streamed from the jungle like giant sparklers exploding all over. Soon, mortars opened up from the jungle area behind that hootch. The enemy threw everything into that graveyard.

Cowboy died in that graveyard. That night in the graveyard, he curled up behind one of the little round grave mounds—the only cover those guys had—and his heart stopped. The corpsman could find no wounds. Chan told me later that they found a small wound, but it wasn't serious enough to kill him. Not far from Cowboy was another young Marine named Sonny, who was hit around eleven times with machine gun bullets and still lived. I heard that Sonny went home and became a Virginia State Congressman. Pat McCrary was wounded beside Sonny and Cowboy that night.

When they wouldn't give Pat his Purple Heart license tag, he started his own investigation and finally discovered that our records had taken a direct hit from a big 122mm rocket in An Hoa Combat Base. All the Marines in the records shack were killed, all of our records destroyed. That news reopened a search for lost records for a lot of the men in Alpha Company, 1st Battalion, 5th Marines.

There was a company gunnery sergeant named Poertner. I never knew him personally, but he told me that he witnessed what I did in the graveyard that night and had written me up for the Silver Star. I had been told by some of the guys, including my A-gunner right after that battle, that they were writing me up for a medal, but I never got it.

When Poertner found out about the records being destroyed, he wrote me up again and submitted it to the Secretary of the Navy. Two weeks later, retired Master Sergeant Poertner died. If he had not written that letter when he did, I would have never gotten the Silver Star. The *Tampa Tribune* had a full-page story with color photo of me holding a machine gun. The large headline read, *"Honored at Last."*

I was being honored as a war hero when the truth was, compared to the Marines I served with, I was nothing but another dumb PFC grunt machine gunner. I was only eighteen in Nam, and a young eighteen at that. I made some choices that I've regretted for the rest of my life. The Lord knows all that. He gave me that Silver Star just to balance all of my failures out in my own mind. He was reminding me that I did some good stuff too. My God is so loving and merciful. He is just amazing.

God bestowed honors on me all the time. I was asked to throw out the first pitch at a Tampa Bay Ray's game. They put photos of me on the giant screen. I was invited to speak all over the place, even the Air Force Academy in Colorado Springs. A Marine Sergeant Major came by the Do Jang to meet me and have me sign a book. He told me that he had won the *Divisional Guns Up! Award*. I had no clue what he was talking about, and he was dumbfounded that I was dumbfounded. Then he told me that the Corps had an award named in honor of me and the book.

I was awarded the Silver Star in front of about 2,000 people at the 1st Marine Division Reunion in Cincinnati. Nancy, Shawn, Bonnie, and my mom were there. Chan was there, and Bob Carrol and a lot of the other guys. They were handing out many awards, and there were a lot of young Marines in the audience. After they read the citation, Commanding General Hagee of the 1st

Marine Division pinned the Star on my dress blues.

When I went back to our table, my daughter said that all these young Marines at tables nearby got excited as they heard the citation. Before my daughter Bonnie finished telling me about their reaction, our table was surrounded by a platoon of young Marines in dress blues. One young man had just been awarded Marine Corps Sergeant of the Year. He did the talking.

"Sir, are you Johnnie Clark?"

"Yes," I said.

"Sir, are you the Johnnie Clark who wrote 'The Book'?"

"The book?"

"Yes, sir. 'The Book.'"

"You mean, Guns Up!?"

"The Book. Yes, sir."

"I wrote it. As a matter of fact, this is Chan sitting here."

Instantly more Marines gathered around our table. Questions were coming from everywhere. Then they all came to attention as General Haggee worked his way through the crowd and looked questioningly at the young Marines.

The sergeant spoke up excitedly. "Sir, this is Johnnie Clark!"

"Yes, Sergeant. I met Mr. Clark a few moments ago."

"Sir, this is the Johnnie Clark that wrote 'The Book'."

This poor general and future commandant of the Marine Corps stood before his men looking like a new recruit. He didn't have a clue what these guys were so excited about. So they decided that he must not have heard them.

"The Book, sir."

"You know."

"Johnnie and Chan!"

"The book."

Finally, General Haggee shook his head and confirmed the obvious. "I'm sorry, men. What book?"

"Guns Up!, General," the sergeant said as a dozen or so echoed the title.

He was absolutely embarrassed. The Marines looked at him as if he had not returned a salute. He turned to me, and I think this combat veteran was red faced.

"My apologies, Mr. Clark. I have not read your book."

There were two Medal of Honor men who were there that night, along with a room full of remarkable Marines, but the only thing these young Marines were interested in was the lance corporal who wrote "The Book." This is how God keeps honoring me and using this book. I knew that the only reason that little book mattered was because it was a witness for Christ, but watching the way the Lord continued to use it was and still just amazes me. It was also more of the Lord's mercy on me. He knew that I could not forgive myself for some terrible sins, but He kept reassuring me that He had.

Later that night in our hotel room Shawn, Bonnie, and Nancy were all laughing about the reaction of all those young Marines. It really was fun to see how much it meant to them. To me, it was very humbling. When someone knocked on the hotel door with three solid knocks, I knew it was a Marine and just assumed it had something to do with *Guns Up!* I opened the door to face a handsome young major in dress greens.

"Mr. Clark?"

"Yes."

"General Haggee requests a copy of your book at your earliest convenience, sir."

"I don't have one with me, Major, but I'll be honored to mail the general a copy."

"That would be outstanding, sir. Here is his address." He handed me the address with no hesitation, having had it already prepared. He saluted and departed.

I mailed a copy of all my books to the General of the 1st Marine Division and got an immediate response from him. It read, "Dear Mr. Clark, I want to thank you for the books and inform you that 'The Book' will be read the instant we finish combat maneuvers here in Korea. I assure you that, if at all possible, I will never be that embarrassed in front of my troops again!"

General Haggee went on to become the Commandant of the Marine Corps and quickly put my books on The Commandant's List of Suggested Reading for All Marines. In the Corps, that's a pretty big deal, and once again I was being honored more than I deserved.

11

GUNNER'S GLORY

In 1999, I had started a new book and pitched the idea to Random House for publishing. It would be the stories of machine gunners from World War II, Korea, and Vietnam. They loved the idea, and soon I was deep into research and trying to get help from every old Marine I knew. I put out a want ad of sorts in Marine publications asking for help in finding Marine gunners and, wow, did I get some incredible men.

I told Ray Hinst and his son Raymond about the new book I was working on. They own Haslam's Book Store, the oldest and best bookstore in the Southeast United States. It's funny how God uses others in our lives. I was delivering books to Haslam's Book Store when I injured my back as a mailman. That finished me as a mailman and led me to being a writer. Haslam's was on my mail route, and I had become friends with the whole family. Old man Haslam and Mrs. Haslam ran the store then and were strong Christians who had worked many missionary trips around the world.

Ray married the Haslams' daughter and started running the store after Mr. and Mrs. Haslam died. He hosted my first book signing when *Guns Up!* came out, and it broke the record for the most books sold at a signing at Haslam's. That started a tradition, and Haslam's Book Store has hosted the first signing for each of my subsequent books.

Ray had been a colonel in the Air Force and has great respect for combat Marines. When he heard about the theme for the new book, he and his son couldn't wait to tell me about an old "Salt" they knew. Raymond's eyes grew wide open with excitement when he grabbed my arm.

"Oh, my God, Johnnie! You have to meet this old Marine machine gunner named Ted Elleston!"

"Johnnie," Ray senior said seriously. "He was with Edson's Raiders on Guadalcanal."

That was all I had to hear but certainly not all they had to tell me. Ray and Raymond took turns telling me the story of this old Marine machine gunner who came into the bookstore all the time. They ended it with this.

"Ted was just in last week and his hand was . . ." Ray started grinning and chuckling so much that his son Raymond took over the story.

"His right hand was all scabbed up and purple."

Ray was still smiling but jumped back into the story. "So I said, 'Hey, Ted, what'd you do to your hand?' And Ted looks at it and says in his deep baritone voice, 'Oh, I had to square this guy away.' So we both look at each other grinning, because Ted is eighty-four years old! Of course I asked what happened. And old Ted says, 'This guy was roughing up this girl down here on the corner, so I had to square him away.'"

Raymond started howling as he took over. "Johnnie, he didn't know it was a pimp. He saw this pimp roughing up one of his prostitutes, and this eighty-four-year-old Marine knocked him out cold and left him lying out on Central Avenue."

Well, I was already in love with this guy when I heard he had served with Edson's Raiders, but now this was "Out-Marine Corps-standing." The two Rays gave me Ted's contact information, and from the first phone conversation, we were brothers. I went to his two-room condo to interview him, but Ted quickly became more than just another war story in the new book.

As weeks and months went by, we shared some deep moments that only combat vets can share. Ted still slept with the hunting knife that he killed a Japanese soldier with on Guadalcanal after his machine gun ran out of ammo and all his grenades were used up. He showed me stains on that old hunting knife and told me the Jap's blood wouldn't go away.

I told Ted my own horror story and that I still slept with a KA-BAR every night. It was not the only similarity we had as Marine machine gunners, and in spite of the difference in age we were kindred spirits. Ted had been shipped off Guadalcanal with combat fatigue and taken to Mare Island Hospital in San Francisco. I told him that I'd also been diagnosed with severe combat fatigue and that I sometimes wondered if I would ever sleep normally again. Ted assured me that I would not. So far, he's right.

Ted was a very tough man, but he was also a strong believer, and we did more than share Napoleon Brandy and sea stories—we shared our faith. Our faith in Christ sealed our friendship until his death. That incredibly brutal battle that Ted was in on Guadalcanal is legendary in the Marine Corps and was the turning point of the war with Japan. It also plays a part in the miracle that this book is about.

The Japanese had won every land battle in the war when the Marines hit the beach on Guadalcanal. They were building an airstrip on the island as a final preparation for the invasion of Australia. If the Marines couldn't take and hold Guadalcanal, Australia was lost. It is difficult for those who don't know history to understand just how dire the situation was in 1942. The war was being lost in Europe, and the Japanese were rolling through the Pacific like a tidal wave. They seemed invincible. California was actually in danger of an invasion if that little island of Guadalcanal could not be taken and held.

The Marines took it and took the air field, but because the Japanese Navy was so strong, it was nearly impossible to get replacements and supplies to them. The Marines were being pounded by Naval gunfire all night and bombed from the air during the day. There was a ridgeline of high ground on the inland edge of the air strip, and whoever held that ridgeline held the airfield. That famous ridgeline became known as Bloody Ridge, though some called it Edson's Ridge. The Marines named the air strip Henderson Field in honor of a Marine hero killed in the battle of Midway.

It was on Bloody Ridge that Ted Elleston's machine gun position was overrun and held by a mere hunting knife and one very tough Marine Raider. The Raiders and the rest of the 5th Marine Regiment were taking heavy casualties holding out on Guadalcanal while the Japanese continued to funnel thousands of troops onto the island for more counter attacks, which seemed destined to overwhelm the Marines.

As I wrote Ted's story, I felt like I was living it. It sounds nuts to a non-Marine, but I was envious. What a fight the Corps put up. The whole battle was amazing. I asked Ted for more leads on the stories of other machine gunners. He didn't hesitate.

"You need to talk to Mitch Paige. He was a machine gunner and came ashore with the 7th

Marines when we finally got some replacements. He was on Bloody Ridge."

"Why does his name sound familiar?"

"Medal of Honor. He's the Marine that Hasbro Toys made the famous G.I. Joe doll after. And boy, we gave him some crap over that! G.I. Joe! As if he was in the bloody Army."

And that was it. That was my introduction to the famous Marine that Hasbro Toys made a doll in honor of, Sergeant Mitchell Paige. I never dreamed that I would get to know Mitchell Paige, let alone share in a miracle with him. But once again, God was guiding me to where He wanted me to go and a mountain He wanted me to climb.

12

SGT. MITCHELL PAIGE

Sgt. Mitchell Paige, a retired colonel, was living in Palm Springs with his wife Marilyn when I first contacted him. If I hadn't been a fellow Marine, I don't believe he would have given me the go-ahead to use this story. Mitch had been taken to the hospital and was pretty weak. It didn't look good and seemed he would never leave the hospital. We conducted phone interviews while he was on his deathbed—when he was strong enough and Marilyn gave the okay. He confirmed the miracle that happened on Guadalcanal and told me every detail. I am adding these excerpts from *Gunner's Glory* with Mrs. Marilyn Paige's approval.

These excerpts from *GUNNER'S GLORY* were taken by permission from Mitchell Paige's own book titled *A Marine Named Mitch* (Wylde & Sons). I highly recommend the book.

Remember that Mitchell Paige is only one of many heroic Marines I've written about. Psalm 121 had no special meaning to me. I have many Bible verses in my books, and I certainly do not remember every verse in every book, especially years after writing it. Did I remember the miracle he told me about on his deathbed? You better believe I remembered it. If a guy tells you a story like that when he's dying, you're gonna remember it. But life goes on, time passes, and it's not as if I went to bed every night dwelling on a story that I had written a couple of years earlier.

* * * * *

SGT. MITCHELL PAIGE
Medal of Honor

Rank and organization: Platoon Sergeant, United States Marine Corps. Place and date: Solomon Islands, 26 October 1942. Entered service at: Pennsylvania. Birth: Charleroi, PA. Citation: For extraordinary heroism and conspicuous gallantry in action above and beyond the call of duty while serving with a company of Marines in combat against enemy Japanese forces in the Solomon Islands on 26 October 1942. When the enemy broke through the line directly in front of his position, Platoon Sergeant Paige, commanding a machine gun section with fearless determination, continued to direct the fire of his gunners until all of his men were either killed or wounded. Alone, against the deadly hail of Japanese shells, he fought with his gun and when it was destroyed, took over another, moving from gun to gun, never ceasing his withering fire against the advancing hordes until reinforcements finally arrived. Then, forming a new line, he dauntlessly and aggressively led a bayonet charge, driving the enemy back and preventing a breakthrough in our lines. His great personal valor and unyielding devotion to duty were in keeping with the highest traditions of the United States Naval Service.

* * * * *

I genuinely liked school. Each day our teacher would lead us in the Pledge of Allegiance to the flag as we stood by our desks. Before sitting she would then read a passage from the Bible. Each day was a different verse but one passage has always remained my favorite. *"I will lift up mine eyes unto the hills, from whence cometh my help. My help cometh from the Lord, which made Heaven and earth. . . ."* It was Psalm 121 and it remains my favorite.

I had wonderful teachers, and we respected them greatly. My teachers were strict, but they taught us faith in God and the Bible. They taught us a love of our country and what our flag stood for and the cost of freedom. They taught us to honor our father and mother. The love of God and country that I learned in the little Camden School always remained with me, even on Guadalcanal.

* * * * *

Days went by and the air raids continued. More and more men were stricken with malaria, but most of them would not leave the lines. We bundled each victim up in anything we had when the chills came, and each Marine would sweat it out until it hit again.

Then I caught malaria, too. It hit so hard that I couldn't move any part of my body except my eyes. I could only look down. If I moved them up toward my forehead, the pain was terrible. If I looked up fast, it felt as though my eyeballs had pressed against a sharp blade. I was going through a bad spell when an air raid came over us. I couldn't move. I laid out and tried to keep from moving my eyes up as bombs began to land around us. One of my men came and sat beside me.

"Get into a foxhole, Marine," I ordered with the strongest voice I could muster. It was a Marine named Wilson B. Faust. He ignored me and began to pray for us. I could hear a string of Jap bombs whistling down on us and since my head was flat on the ground, I could tell by each explosion that we were right in the bomb pattern. The explosions were getting closer. Wilson kept praying. A bomb landed just to our right and I knew the next one would be a direct hit on Faust and me. He continued praying out loud, and the next bomb dropped into a soggy part of the jungle a few yards away from us. Mud covered both of us as the bomb created a huge crater. I looked up at Faust.

"We were saved by your fervent prayer, Faust." He nodded and I asked him to join me in reciting the 121st Psalm together. We did and I felt close to the Lord. I felt that peace that passes understanding.

* * * * *

On the way back to the knoll, I saw the movement of Japanese troops on the ridge just above Major Conoley's position, the exact position that I had raked with grazing fire earlier. I fired Kelly's and Totman's full belt of 250 rounds into that area. Once again the rounds were ricocheting over Conoley's head, but they had no way of knowing that I was doing the firing. We advanced back across the ridge. Some of the Japanese began falling back. To my right I saw that several Japs were crawling awkwardly across the knoll with their rifles in the crooks of their arms. My heart froze as I realized they were crawling toward one of my guns, which was now out in the open and unmanned.

I ran for the gun. From the gully area several Japanese guns spotted me and swiveled to rake me with fire. Their fire brought more fire as snipers in the trees tried to bring me down. Mortar shells began bursting around me as I ran to that gun. An enemy soldier with a Nambu machine gun saw me coming and jumped up to race me to the prize. I got there first and jumped into a hole behind the gun. The Japanese soldier dropped to the ground with his Nambu machine gun less than twenty-five yards away, point-blank range. He opened fire. I turned my machine gun on the enemy soldier only to realize it was not loaded. I scooped a partial belt of .30-caliber ammo out of the dirt, my fingers bleeding and slippery, and fumbled frantically trying to load the gun. I got the belt in and moved to pull back the bolt.

Suddenly an extraordinary sensation came over me. I tried desperately to reach forward to pull the bolt handle back to load the gun, but I felt as though I were in a vise. The Japanese machine gunner was blazing away at me, but something was keeping me from moving forward. As if some invisible force held me back. In spite of what I know should have been a life-and-death state of hopeless panic, I was completely relaxed and felt as though I were sitting peacefully in a park. I could feel a strange, warm impression between my chin and my Adam's apple, which I knew were bullets. The Japanese Nambu gunner finished his thirty-round magazine at the precise moment that I suddenly fell forward over the gun as if suddenly being released from some invisible hold. I pulled the bolt handle back and swung it at the enemy gunner. I killed him. For the rest of my life I would think about this moment. I never wanted to relate this experience to anyone because I did not ever want to have anyone question it. Jesus Christ and I know exactly what happened.

* * * * *

As I gathered up my backpack, I had a question in my mind and heart that I had to have an answer to. I walked over to the body of the Japanese Nambu machine gunner and shoved his body over the bank with my foot. The man who had shot a full load of thirty rounds at my head at point-blank range. Those rounds shaved my chin and throat at the exact moment when I could not move forward to pull back the bolt and load the machine gun . . . that moment when something held me like I was in an inconceivable, supernatural grip.

I laid my pack down and crouched to look through the sights of the Nambu. I saw that there was absolutely no doubt. It was too incredible to understand, and I mumbled to myself, "Lord, he had me dead center. How could he miss me with thirty rounds, thirty rounds that should have gone right into my left ear?" My pinky finger was bleeding badly from parrying away the Jap bayonet. It was nearly severed. I reached over and grabbed my pack to try to find something to wrap my bleeding finger. A small Gideon Bible fell out of it, open on the ground. The book seemed to open, though I felt no wind. I looked down at it. Letters on one page stood out as if they were larger than all the other words in that small Bible. There was still very little light and those words seemed to be larger, almost lit up compared to everything around them. They looked to be an inch larger than the rest of the page. I stared for a few moments in awe. It was Proverbs 3:5-6. Then I read those words. "Trust in the Lord with all your heart and do not lean on your own understanding. In all your ways acknowledge Him, and He will make your paths straight." I picked up the Bible and my pack and found a spot to sit and think. My mom's last words to me when I joined the Corps rang out like a church bell, "Mitch, trust in the Lord with all your heart." I believe there is no doubt that this was a word from the Lord God Almighty. I told no one about the incident. I didn't want the guys to think I'd gone nuts. But it is true.

* * * * *

This is what I wrote at the end of the Mitchell Paige story.

Col. Mitchell Paige and his lovely wife Marilyn gave me his story through interviews and e-mails, but the majority of this American legend's story came right out of his own book, "*A Marine Named Mitch*" by Mitchell Paige (Wylde & Sons). The photos are used with permission from his book. Mitchell Paige is one of the finest patriots I've ever had the honor of speaking with. He's as brilliant as he is brave. He honors the Lord Jesus Christ in the way he lives and the way he speaks. I pray that God will bless our country with more men like Mitchell Paige. When he spoke with me about his own personal miracle on Guadalcanal, I was touched to my very soul. He told me he was hesitant to even tell the other men what had happened for fear that they would think he was nuts. He and Marilyn told me the story so that God would be honored and people would know the

165

truth about what happened to this hero on Guadalcanal. Mitchell Paige spoke the humble truth, and his story is a blessing to anyone who hears it.

And here is what I wrote in the dedication just before the book went to Random House.

As I was writing the dedication for this book, I received a phone call telling me that the legend, Col. Mitchell Paige, had died. America has lost one of her great sons. My sadness is tempered with the knowledge of where Mitch is right now. Semper fi, Marine.

*   *   *   *   *

Writing about Mitchell Paige and getting to know him was a great honor. I want to remind the reader that this great man confirmed the miracle on Guadalcanal while he was dying in a hospital. If you think a man like Mitchell Paige would lie about something dealing with God almighty while on his death bed, you probably should stop reading this book and start praying.

As amazing as this story and this man were, there were six other incredible stories in that book about some great Marines, and as a writer, I got lost in each man's story. Once the book was finished, I never thought much about those stories. After I finish a book, I never look at it again. If I start re-reading my own books, I end up wanting to rewrite them, so I've learned better over the years. Besides, you get sort of emotionally worn out and ready to move on to the next one.

13

GRAYBEARD MOUNTAIN

It had been a couple of years since I wrote the story of Sergeant Mitchell Paige and a couple of years since I had thought about it. The only war story on my mind most of the time was my own. I relived ambushes many nights and sometimes woke up terrified and fumbling for my KA-BAR thinking I was in hand-to-hand combat. It was not a shock to Nancy when I kicked her or told her it was her watch or grabbed her in the middle of the night. She was afraid to wake me because she wasn't sure what I might do.

When I didn't sleep, I was grouchy all day, and I guess I was depressed. My son Shawn was now at Florida State University, and I really missed him. When my baby girl, Bonnie, moved to a dorm in Tampa to go to USF, I got very depressed. It was hard on Nancy too. One of the ways I had always been able to fight depression was by training. I had recovered from back surgery and was able to train again. Soon my left knee, which has some shrapnel in it, started giving me trouble. It ended up being just a torn meniscus, but it was another knee surgery, which meant another halt to my training. That hurt the Do Jang business because the students who paid to train paid to train with me.

We kept the old Bible study going somehow. The ranks would grow and diminish, but there was always a core group that had bonded together for many years. Ann Owen, George Leonard, Chris and Benita Pagac, Terry O'Grady, Nancy and me. Sometimes, my old Pastor Phil Engelman and his wife, Sue, would drop in for a visit. That was always special because Pastor Engelman is a wonderful Bible teacher, and with Phil there I didn't have to be the study leader.

It was a Thursday night Bible Study in early August, 2004. Phil and Sue had shown up, and Phil led the study. When the study ended, I unloaded a bunch of crap on Phil, as I always did. He's the best listener in the world and, for me, the most trusted spiritual adviser on earth. It was pretty obvious to Phil that I was in need of spiritual repair.

"Johnnie, when was the last time you were alone with the Lord?"

I chuckled with fatigue. "This morning."

"No. I mean when was the last time you went somewhere to be alone with the Lord?"

I thought about it and was stumped. I finally said, "I don't think I've gone somewhere to be alone with the Lord since I was a little kid in West Virginia. I used to go up on Spring Hill Mountain and talk to God."

"I've been doing the most fascinating study on being alone with God," he said. "Sue and I have now made this a vital part of our lives."

Phil grabbed up a Bible and opened it, searching for verses. He found one he was looking for and read it. It was *Mark 1:35. "In the early morning, while it was still dark, Jesus got up, left the house and went away to a secluded place, and was praying there."*

Phil quickly flipped to another verse and read, *"But Jesus Himself would often slip away to the wilderness and pray."* That was *Luke 5:16.* And I really like this one in Luke, Johnnie." He turned a few pages. *"It was at this time that He went off to the mountain to pray, and He spent the whole night in prayer to God. And when day came, He called His disciples to Him and chose twelve of them, whom He also named as apostles."* (Luke 6:12).

The idea of getting away sounded awfully good.

"You know something, Phil, that sounds great. Nancy and I could really use a vacation like that."

"No! I mean you all by yourself. No wife, no kids, no friends, just you and the Lord. Go somewhere for a few days to be alone with Jesus Christ. Powerful things can happen to a man when he sacrifices his time with family and friends to be completely alone with God. Do you have someplace you could go to stay for a few days, maybe a week? Away from people."

I looked at Nancy to see what she thought of the idea.

"Tony and Jane Horning live in Black Mountain, North Carolina now," she said. "They might know of a cabin."

Phil put his hand on my shoulder. "I truly believe you need to do this. Just go away for a week to be alone with God."

Phil gave me a couple more passages from scripture dealing with being alone with God. I knew or had read them before, and I knew that Jesus did this all the time. It was clear to me right away—I had to do this at least once in my life. I called Tony Horning that night. Tony Horning had been the principal of Northside Christian School in St. Pete and had trained with me for years. He was my senior black belt master. Tony and Jane were old Grace Bible people too. Tony had moved to Black Mountain to open a new charter school with his wife Jane a couple of years earlier.

As soon as I told Tony what the plan was, he chuckled. "That's funny," he said. "Must be the Lord's will."

"Why?"

"Jane's friend is married to this doctor who works at Duke University. They own a little two-story cabin in Montreat, and we look after it for them. It's not in deep woods, but it's alone enough to get black bears on the porch."

I flew up that week and rented a car. I drove to the Hornings' house, and they led me to the

Black Mountain grocery store for supplies. I got some TV dinners, coffee, water, and a couple of bottles of Merlot. I followed them through the small town of Black Mountain and on a couple of miles to Montreat.

My first impression was disappointment. I wanted to be out in the woods alone. Montreat was a little resort area in a valley between mountains. It was sparsely populated, but it wasn't alone enough for me. We turned off of the two-lane blacktop road and crossed a small bridge, then went up a dirt-and-gravel road. Tony pulled off the road to the right, and I pulled in behind him. To our left there was a little park and tennis courts situated between the main road and the dirt road. This certainly didn't look remote to me. Half a mile up the road, there were a couple of shops and Lake Susan, where tourists could rent canoes. There was also an old resort hotel where the dirt-and-gravel road led back to the blacktop road. It was called Assembly Inn.

I had no idea where the two-lane blacktop road that went through the town led to. I had never been there in my life, but it was obvious that there were some million-dollar homes nestled in the hills on both sides of that road. Montreat College is situated near the entrance and there's a lovely little church made of Carolina river rocks in Montreat. It was Tony and Jane's church, and they told me that it was where Billy Graham was married.

My cabin was hard to see from the road. It was about a hundred yards up steep steps and built onto the side of a fairly steep hill. They got me settled in, and I told them not to be insulted, but I didn't want to visit with them on this trip. I had to be alone. They understood. They gave me the lowdown on the area, directions to the various spots in Black Mountain, and some tips about the place, like making sure the garbage can lid was tight because of the bears. Then we said our goodbyes, and I tried to get acclimated to being alone.

The cabin wasn't out in the deep woods as I had wanted, but it was plenty alone. It was a getaway for the Duke doctor and his family and didn't look like it had been used in a long time. It smelled musty, and the windows were all either nailed shut or fixed so they would open only halfway. The woods were thick enough so that I couldn't see any other houses, but I was close enough to the road to go down and take a walk if I wanted to wander up to Lake Susan.

The cabin had a living room, bathroom, and kitchen with stairs leading up to a back door and laundry room. There were two steps up from the laundry room and bathroom to the two bedrooms. The back door at the head of the stairs just below the laundry room was hilarious. It opened into a boulder in the side of the mountain. There were some spider webs in the corners, and it smelled moldy, but the place was actually much nicer than I had expected.

That first night started off quietly. I had the upstairs bedroom window slightly open. All I could hear were those pleasant sounds that the woods make. You know the sounds we all enjoy, like those from the crickets or frogs. I was just a little on edge, to tell you the truth. I couldn't bring my KA-BAR or my .45 caliber pistol on the plane, so it was uncomfortable at first. I finally went downstairs to the kitchen and found the biggest knife they had and kept it on the nightstand by my bed.

I guess it was around 1 a.m. when I heard a noise against the side of the house. I went down the first small flight of stairs to the back door but could see nothing. I went downstairs to check the front door. I looked out but saw nothing, so went back to bed. I'd started to doze off when I heard some voices coming from the road down below. I was up, awake and angry. Immediately the thumps on the side of the cabin and the voices below were connected as far as I was concerned. I went downstairs again, flipped on the porch light, and stepped onto the porch holding the knife.

No one was there. The voices were gone. I went back to bed and slept my usual form of sleep—half-awake. Soon, something thumped against the side of the house again, and I was up. I could see nothing from the upstairs window. I heard voices from the road again. So down I went. This time I walked all the way down the steps to the road.

No one was there. I climbed back up to the cabin and went back to bed. But now I couldn't sleep at all. Having to fear that someone was sneaking up on me made me an angry man. I was sleepy and grumpy that next day, and that next night was more of the same.

By the third night, I was seriously ticked off and convinced that someone was doing this to give me a hard time. I found some six-penny nails, a hammer and boards and decided to set up a Nam-style ambush with a couple of punji-pits. When someone stepped on one of these I'd hear 'em scream, and then I was gonna' beat the crap out of them.

That night I slept a little better just knowing that I had some sort of perimeter. It was around midnight when I heard voices down on the road. Then I heard a girl laughing, but it was coming from the tennis courts, not close to the cabin. I went back to sleep figuring it was just some college kids having a few beers or something. Montreat College was a few miles away.

I guess I was half asleep and half-awake when something hit the front door downstairs. That was it. I was really ticked off. I sprang out of bed with the knife and headed downstairs, nearly killing myself as I missed a step or two. I hit the outside light and bounded out onto the porch. There was no one there. It was dark and silent in the woods around the cabin. No movement could be heard anywhere. I couldn't figure out how these clowns had avoided my booby-traps when they stepped up onto the porch.

I went back inside, turned off the light and waited with only the screen-door closed. I must have sat there an hour, but nothing happened. I finally locked the door, went back upstairs to bed, and fell asleep exhausted. You probably figured out already that these nightly noises were bears! But my mindset wasn't on bears, and for whatever goofy reason, it didn't dawn on me until days later that those guys invading my perimeter were covered with fur.

The next morning I got up feeling a little more rested but still frustrated. I had some coffee and something to eat out on the porch and started reading my Bible. For the first time in three days, this time alone with God finally felt good. Here I was, sitting on a porch swing breathing the cool mountain air and alone with the Lord. This was the way the trip was supposed to be. It had been three days of utter frustration, but I told myself things would be good now.

I removed the booby traps just to be safe, then I went back inside to get another cup of coffee. When I returned to the porch, a man was coming up the steps from the road with a large bucket filled with various tools and extension cords. He came up onto the porch and introduced himself.

"Hi, I'm Tom Spangler. I'm the owner. I'm going to be doing some work on the downstairs bathroom—got some termite damage. I'll be using the porch here to cut some two-by-fours."

That was it! I went upstairs, and he went to work. The guy sounded like an entire construction crew. After a couple of hours listening to saws and hammers, I was finished. This trip was an absolute disaster. I'd left my family and business to fly to North Carolina, spending money we didn't have, just to be a frustrated idiot. My plan was to make no cell phone calls on this trip, but it was time to vent. I called Nancy.

I really try to not curse, and I don't cuss much, but the truth is, I probably spit out a few four-letter words as I told Nancy what a total failure this trip had been. I vented and angrily listed my grievances in a loud voice to be heard over the saws and hammers. When I told her I had set up some booby-traps, she was worried and knew my frustration level was serious. That's when she said something that I needed to hear and that I now know came straight from God.

"Johnnie, you don't sound good. You need to go for a long walk."

I paused in my rant and thought about it for a moment. "Yeah. A walk. You're right. I'll call you later." I threw the cell phone on the bed.

I headed downstairs, passed the one-man construction crew, continued down to the road, and headed to the right. I walked past the lake, past the mostly vacant hotel, and followed the road for a long way. There were very few cars if any on that road. Not many people lived that far outside of Montreat. I kept walking uphill until the blacktop ended and the road became red dirt and gravel. I can't swear to how long I had been walking, but it was a fairly decent hike.

Black clouds were rolling in over the mountains, and it looked like a pretty good storm was coming. I reached a place where the road seemed to end at a small leveled-off gravel parking area. There were no cars and no humans. There was a sign that read "Graybeard Mountain, Elevation 5,408 feet." Near that sign was another sign with a lot of warnings. "Be careful of bears . . . Always hike with another climber . . . Bring water and cell phone . . . The warnings went on and on. . . .

I had none of the above and was wearing shorts and a T-shirt. I looked down at my tennis shoes and the fresh scar from my recent knee surgery, shrugged, and headed across a wooden bridge spanning a fast-moving stream. There had been an earlier rain on the mountain, and the ground was wet. The climb was steep and rocky. A few hundred feet up, I paused and realized this was a serious climb and that I was really out in the woods. I searched around until I found a perfect staff, about six-foot long. I could fight with a staff, I thought, then laughed. As if that would help if I ran into a bear. But it did help my knee with the steep climb.

As I struggled up that mountain trail, a lot of the stress and frustration from the last three days melted away. For the first time, I really was alone with God. There wasn't a soul on this mountain. Huge black clouds continued rolling in overhead. Thunder was echoing from far away like the distant sounds of B-52 strikes. Only an idiot would be on this mountain with this storm coming in, I thought. But I kept going.

The sound of a waterfall came from somewhere up ahead. I didn't know how far up I was, but I'd been climbing enough to break a good sweat when the trail came to a beautiful mountain stream. The stream looked like one of the old cigarette commercials. It was too wide to cross without getting wet, but there was a decent sized boulder in the middle, so I stepped out onto a couple of little rocks and made it to the boulder and plopped down to enjoy the beauty around me.

I sat there for some time listening to the waterfall somewhere below me. I started talking to God. I wasn't really praying. I was just talking to Him the way you would talk to a friend or maybe your dad. Yeah, I was murmuring and complaining. Of course, I can't remember everything I said, but do remember the most important part very clearly.

"What am I doing here, Jesus?"

I sometimes call him Jesus, sometimes Lord, when I talk to God, and by either name, I was fairly adamant because I was still just a little frustrated with this whole effort. Then I said, "What's the point? What the crap am I doing here, sitting on a mountain in North Carolina all alone? Why am I here?"

Naturally there was no thunderous answer from the storm clouds above, and I decided to stop talking and pray. I prayed for a while and tried my best to figure out why I was there and what exactly the Lord was trying to teach me. I started thinking about the attributes of God. Then I started thinking about some of the great men in the Bible. I always thought of David because I really relate to David, and God called him a man after God's own heart. Then thoughts of good old Moses came to me and what the Lord said about him. The Lord called Moses the most humble man on earth. God loves a humble man and hates pride. As a matter of fact, humility is one of the Lord's favorite character traits.

When those thoughts went through my head, it was like a lightbulb turned on. I knew now why I was in the middle of nowhere all alone. God wanted me to learn humility. I sat there staring at the fresh scar on my knee and thought about my personality. This mountain was 5,408 feet to the top, and I was naturally going to climb all the way, bad knee or not, because that's the way Johnnie Clark is wired. Here was the perfect example of being a prideful jackass. Humility! God wanted to teach me to be more humble.

"Okay, Lord. I won't climb another step." I got to my feet and made my way across a couple of rocks to keep from getting wet, then started back down the mountain. I was feeling pretty good about my decision as I headed down that rugged trail. It just felt like I was pleasing the Lord, and maybe I had just a little relief, as if some mystery had been solved. The mystery of what in the world

Johnnie Clark was doing on some mountain alone in North Carolina.

Going downhill was much more treacherous than coming up had been, but my attitude was much better. The narrow trail was steep, very rocky and slippery, and I used that staff to try to keep from busting my rear end. All of my frustration seemed to have evaporated as I concentrated on not breaking an ankle or worse.

I had gone about five hundred feet and was stepping off a rocky ledge. So I was in mid-step in midair at about a 45-degree angle downhill with my left foot about a foot and a half off of the ground. The surgery had been to my left knee, so I was naturally bracing for the jar as I came down, trying not slip.

When I finally decided to write this book I knew that this part of my story was going to sound insane. And I couldn't blame anyone for thinking this guy must have some shrapnel in the brain or had been free sparring one too many times in the old Do Jang. But in spite of sounding like I've gone over the edge, I swear before God Almighty that this is true.

I was in mid-step with one foot off of the ground and leaning forward in midair preparing to catch myself with the staff so I wouldn't break my neck or knee when I landed, and at that instant, I was suddenly frozen. I couldn't fall forward, and I certainly couldn't move in any other direction, considering I was at a 45-degree angle heading downhill.

I didn't feel fear, and I guess I was in a bit of shock but completely aware of what was happening. It is impossible to fully explain something like this, but in spite of how absolutely strange or even unworldly this was, I was totally at peace. I was completely and utterly at the mercy of whatever held me in place. I don't know what weightlessness feels like, but if since I must choose a term to explain the feeling of being suspended and held in place by some invisible force, then I guess weightless is as good as any other.

I was held there totally aware of my surroundings but unable to do anything. I was aware of every breath I took. I was in awe, but with a sense of a peace that transcends explanation. I don't know how long I was frozen in midair like that, but it was long enough for a million thoughts to go through my head. Not fearful thoughts. It was as though I were being held in some supernatural yet gentle grip. When I was finally released, I fell forward downhill quite a few steps before I got my balance, and then I twirled around with the staff looking uphill and ready to defend myself. Why defensive when I had never felt such wonder and peace and tranquility in my life? I don't know. I guess it just shows what a fool I can be. There was nothing there. There wasn't a soul on that mountain but me. I knew what had happened. Only God could do that! I was overwhelmed and fell to my knees. I knew it was God Almighty, and I asked out loud from my knees, "What do you want from me, Lord?"

And then He said in a clear audible voice, **"Get up, Johnnie. Johnnie, I want you to walk a little farther with Me."**

And there it was. Anyone who reads this is free to think what they want. I wouldn't blame anyone for thinking the person who wrote this is a fruitcake. But it's the truth, and I'll swear it on the Bible. As a matter of fact, I have sworn it on the Bible. If somebody wants to pay for it, I'll be more than happy—I'll be giddy—to take a lie-detector test. It was not a voice inside my head or some emotional feeling in my heart. It was audible. It was out loud! It was a real voice. It was Jesus Christ.

The voice was overflowing with love. Don't ask me to explain how a voice can be audible love but it was. It was beautiful and clear and calm and filled me with such awe that I could only say, "Yes, Lord."

Listen, to this day, I wish I could have started asking questions or could have just had some sort of conversation, but I could not. All I could do was say, "Yes, Lord."

I got to my feet and started walking back up that mountain. I would have walked all the way to California. I guess I was in some state of shock, but I was perfectly aware of what I was doing. As a matter of fact, it would be impossible for me to be more alert and aware than I was during that climb. I just kept climbing up that trail. I finally came to the mountain stream with the big boulder in the center where I had prayed and made the decision about humility. I made my way to the boulder and kept going on across to the other side of the stream and then continued uphill.

I climbed and never uttered another word. Somehow, I just knew that I was to keep climbing until God stopped me. I don't remember thinking or wondering or even questioning, I had one single goal at that moment, and that goal was to climb until God said something or did something.

It was about another five hundred feet up the mountain after crossing the stream when I came to a big boulder on the right of the trail with a large plaque embedded in the face. The Lord never said anything audible to me again. That was the one and only time so far in my sixty-seven years on earth. But this boulder was where He was leading me. I knew it without asking.

The plaque had been placed in the side of that boulder by some group from Montreat. It was the beginning of *Psalm 121*.

"I LIFT MINE EYES UNTO THE MOUNTAINS, FROM WHENCE COMETH MY HELP? MY HELP COMES FROM THE LORD WHO MADE HEAVEN AND EARTH."

I knelt down and began to pray and cry with absolute joy. I have no clue what I prayed. I was so blown away by what had just happened to me that my mind was going a dozen different directions, and every direction was exciting. I felt like a little kid. All my life I believed in God, but it was no longer just by faith. He actually called me by name. There is no way to write something like this without feeling special and without knowing that it sounds arrogant.

I've been wondering why God allowed me to experience this miracle ever since it happened. Hardly a day goes by when I don't think about it and wonder about it. I wonder if I failed Him by not using this incredible miracle to change some aspect of my life or by not shouting it from rooftops. This happened on August 26, 2004. I am now writing this book on August 29, 2016. It's taken twelve years for me to decide to write this. I just wasn't sure if I was supposed to. Now, as I reread and rewrite and go over my editor's notes on this book, it is 2019.

My editor wrote me a note on this page and she nailed it on the head. "Johnnie, I feel like the chapter ends abruptly. Like there needs to be some conclusion to the question you just raised….should you have done something sooner? And maybe you don't know the answer. To me, I feel like God works in His timing, and you wrote the book when you knew you were supposed to."

I'm afraid my answer is, I just don't know.

JOHNNIE CLARK ON GRAYBEARD

14

WHAT'S IT MEAN?

When I came down off Graybeard Mountain, I had one very spiritual spring to my step. I just couldn't wait to call Nancy and tell her. By the time I made it to the cabin, the owner was gone. I found my cell phone and called Nancy immediately. It was clear right away that I didn't even know how to tell my wife about this without sounding crazy.

I can't imagine what it must have sounded like to Nancy or what she thought, but she at least pretended to believe me. When I finished the call, I got my Bible and looked up *Psalm 121*. I read it over and over and just giggled. I had to talk about this. I ran down the hill to my rental car and raced through Montreat and into Black Mountain. I found my way to Tony and Jane's house.

When I pulled up into their steep driveway, there was another car there with Florida tags. It was just another weird moment during a very weird day. An old friend named Gary Ripple was heading back to Florida after a trip and had just stopped in to visit Tony and Jane. He and Tony were sitting on the porch. Gary was the music minister at Grace Bible, my old church. Nancy and I now went to Calvary Chapel.

I got out of the car and ran up onto the porch. It would probably be better if Tony and Gary wrote this part of the story, but their basic reaction to my arrival and excitement was summed up by Tony like this. "Johnnie, you looked like a guy who had just seen the 'burning bush.'"

I started blurting out the whole story like a kid hopped up on speed. They told me that my face was red, and it sure wasn't sunburn. I rambled excitedly through the story, pausing at one point to tell both of them that I would swear this was the truth on a Bible. I told Tony to get a Bible, and I swore on it. Who knows what was going through their minds as they listened to this story.

Tony is one of the most loyal friends I have, and he knows me well. He believed me. Gary doesn't know me as well, and I didn't know what he thought. Like I've said from the beginning, I don't know if I'd believe a guy telling me a story like that. The only thing going for me was this: Why would I make it up? I was frozen in midair as if I'd been caught in a Star Trek tractor-beam! God spoke out loud to me and called me by name and led me to a rock on a mountain in North Carolina with *Psalm 121* on it? My story was too ridiculous and sort of pointless.

At that time, nothing about Mitchell Paige had entered my mind. I had written *Gunner's Glory* a couple of years earlier and during this mind-blowing experience, I didn't care about or think about anything except what had just happened to me.

I asked Tony to climb up the mountain with me to see the boulder and the Bible verse. Gary had to be heading on back to Florida. I wanted to climb back up right then to show Tony, but he was too smart for that. He said that we'd run out of daylight, and climbing at night was a sure way to break your neck.

His phone was ringing bright and early the next morning. Tony and I went back up that mountain. I was excited and maybe just a little nervous. If that boulder with the Bible verse wasn't there, I told Tony that he needed to have me put away in some quiet rest home. This whole thing was so far off the chart that it was hard to not doubt myself. Was I nuts? If that boulder and verse were not there, then it meant my mind was gone. That was a scary thought. It wasn't that I was not sure that it had happened, but it was just so unbelievable.

It's not like climbing Everest, but Graybeard is a bit more work than going for a jog. When we got to the place where God froze me, I tried to show Tony exactly what happened. It was easy to see that I could not have stopped myself in midair halfway off that ledge as I stepped or sort of jumped downhill. We kept going until we reached the mountain stream, crossed the rock where I had paused to pray about humility, and then went on up another five hundred feet or so.

There it was! I wasn't crazy. The big boulder with these words: *"I lift mine eyes to the mountains, from whence cometh my help? My help comes from the Lord who made heaven and earth...”*

Tony led us in prayer. I cried again. And I think Tony did too. Just for the record, Master Tony Horning is not just a professor and a brilliant musician. He's built like a linebacker. We have photographs in the Do Jang of Tony breaking four two-inch slabs of concrete. He's the guy I want in a foxhole with me if my life's on the line. He's no sissy and he's no fool. I'll match his intellect with anyone's at Harvard or Yale.

As we came back down the mountain, we stopped where God held me. Tony suggested building an altar of rocks to the Lord like the Israelites did when God gave them a miracle at the Jordan River. So we stopped right there and built a little pyramid of rocks to mark the spot and honor God. My heart was overflowing with thanks and joy.

We started back down again, and the question of why God had done it was all we could talk about. Was there some reason for God to bless me like that? Did He do it just because He loves me? What should I do now? Did this mean I should get ready for something?

We both wondered, and I would be a liar if I didn't admit that I fantasied that it might have something to do with my book, *Guns Up!*. I'd been working very hard on a screenplay with a movie director named John Dahl. John had recently finished another film, *The Great Raid,* and had contacted me. He wanted to do a Vietnam War movie and had read *Guns Up!*. He had me out to Hollywood to screen *The Great Raid,* and it was very exciting. I was in a big theater with one other person, Burt Elias, who had been the Associate Producer on *First Blood* with Sylvester Stalone. There were guards at the doors of the theater so that no one else could see it before it was released.

John Dahl was very sympathetic to Nam vets and believed no other men in American history had won every battle and come home to such disgraceful treatment. Scott Chestnut was John's friend and was an editor on John's movies. Scott gave John *Guns Up!* and told him this would make a great movie. John loved the book and asked his brother-in-law, who was a Nam vet, what he thought about it. His brother-in-law had already read it and told him it was the real deal.

John contacted me after that, and we started working on the script. Now, as Tony and I walked down the mountain, we could not help but wonder if the Lord was going to actually give me a movie. I told you, my mind was going in every direction. We reached the bottom of Graybeard and drove back to my cabin. We said our good-byes because I wanted to resume being alone with the Lord. For the next three days, I was on a spiritual high like never in my life. I memorized *Psalm 121* and went back up that mountain every day until I flew home.

When I got home, I couldn't wait to tell Nancy the story in person. I had to see her reaction! I had to know that she believed me. I told her every single detail all the way home from the airport. I dropped my suitcase in the living room and started telling her again. Nancy is not an excitable person. She's so flat-line, she drives me crazy, and I needed a reaction to this story. As I gave her more details, she calmly walked to our front door, opened it, and retrieved the mail. I was ready to strangle her.

There was a small package in the mail, and Nancy started opening it.

I couldn't stand it. I yelled out very loudly, "Are you listening to me? I'm telling you about the most incredible thing that has ever happened to me on earth, and you're checking the frickin' mail!"

She ignored me. She seemed stunned as she studied the small book she had pulled out of the package. She opened the first page. At this point Nancy really was in danger of being strangled. That's when she looked at me sort of funny, maybe a little scared, and asked, "Tell me again exactly what Jesus said to you?"

I blinked and blurted, "Walk a little farther with Me. Johnnie get up. Johnnie, I want you to walk a little farther with me."

"Johnnie. . ." Nancy's voice was suddenly trembling. "This is getting really weird." She held up the little book for me to read the title. There, on the cover of the book that had shown up in our mail at that precise moment, were the words,

WALK A LITTLE FARTHER WITH ME.

The book was from an outfit called Missionary Ventures. I had donated money to them over the years, but in all the years I sent in contributions, they had never once sent me any literature. That's why I like them—all the money went to missions and not to endless mailings. But now, on this day, they sent me that book.

"That's not all," Nancy said as she read the first sentence in the book. "My wife Nancy loves to shop."

Now we were both covered with goose bumps. I can't be positive, but I think I got home on a Thursday, and we had Bible study. It may have been the next night. As soon as our little group was seated and it was time to start the study, I told them I had something incredible to report and then just started blurting out the whole thing.

Even before the story was finished, Chris Pagac was opening his Bible and searching for something. Then he interrupted me.

"Johnnie, what was that verse again?"

"Psalm121:1. 'I will lift up my eyes to the mountains; From whence shall my help come? My help comes from the Lord, Who made heaven and earth. "

Chris smiled and shook his head. "That verse was in your last book! I'm sure of it. Have you got a copy of *Gunner's Glory?*"

I went into my bedroom and found a copy of the book and rushed back to the living room and handed it to Chris. He flipped through and found it pretty quickly.

"Here! Here it is on page sixty-six. It was Mitchell Paige's favorite Bible verse. You wrote it out." He handed me the book, and we passed it around to the group. Everyone was a little shocked, no one more than I was. I had no clue that that verse had been in my last book until that moment. The honest truth was, I had not thought about *Gunner's Glory* at all.

The book came back around to Chris, and as we all started talking about how bizarre and incredible this miracle was and what it might mean. And then, Chris spoke up again.

"I knew it! Look, Johnnie." He held out the book to me. "*Psalm 121*. It's in there again. When Mitchell Paige and his Christian buddy were about to die and the bomb sucked into the mud and they prayed together, they prayed *Psalm 121*."

I looked, and sure enough, there it was again. Now I was beginning to think about and remember all that Mitchell Paige had told me. Not until that moment did it dawn on me that what had happened to me on Graybeard Mountain was exactly what had happened to Mitchell Paige on Guadalcanal. It all came back to me—everything he told me about being frozen or held in place, the total peace he felt in spite of the Japanese soldier aiming and firing thirty rounds at point blank range.

For the first time I realized this amazing connection to Mitchell Paige. By the end of the

Bible study, I think the guys believed me. They could see this was too incredible to make up, never mind the fact that there was no reason to make up such a crazy story.

The next morning as I prayed, I kept asking the Lord if this was real. I couldn't help doubting myself and wondering what or why this was happening. I flat out asked God if it was real or if I was going nuts. I came into the living room and told Nancy what I had prayed, and we sat on our couch and had a serious talk about the whole thing. Why would God talk to me out loud? Why would God Almighty allow a piece of dirt like me to hear His voice? Why would He call me by name? Moses or King David or the Apostles, but come on—Johnnie Clark? It was too much for even me to believe, and yet I knew it happened. Nancy had no answers either, but she believed me . . . I think. We heard the mailman and kept talking about it as I went to the front door, opened it, and pulled out the mail.

There was a package from a total stranger. I think it had come from out west somewhere. I opened it and showed Nancy. It was a book with a letter from the author. I read the letter to Nancy. The guy was a big fan of my books and was asking me to write a little blurb that he could put on the cover of his book. I was flattered that anyone would think a blurb from Johnnie Clark would mean anything. I opened the cover, and on the very first page was *Psalm 121*.

I showed Nancy, and we were both speechless.

After a little while, I said, "Nancy, this is really getting weird."

We were quiet for a few minutes and then I asked her, "Do you think this has anything to do with *Guns Up!*?"

All she could do was shrug.

I got on my computer and wrote a letter to John Dahl, the movie director. John was a Christian, and I trusted him. I told him everything, including what had happened since I came home from the mountain. I ended the email with this: "John, I know I must sound crazy, and I don't blame you if you think I've gone nuts, but I swear to you that all of this has happened to me, and Nancy and I have no clue what it means." I hit "Send."

Within only a couple of minutes I got an email from a guy named Scott Chestnut. I didn't know this guy, although I did recognize his name because Scott was a good friend of John Dahl and worked as an editor on *The Great Raid*. He was the guy who first read *Guns Up!* and gave it to John. He wrote me this:

Dear Johnnie,

You don't know me, but I am John Dahl's longtime friend and worked behind the camera and as an editor on *The Great Raid*. John didn't think you would mind me writing you this. He just forwarded me your letter, and I had to tell you that "You are not crazy. I absolutely believe that all of this has happened to you."

Here is why I know you are telling the truth. My wife and I are Christians, but my mother-in-law is not saved. We have prayed for her for a long time, but she has no interest in the Lord. Last night she came to us and told us that she has terminal cancer. She asked us for prayer. We prayed, and my wife told me that she got a word from the Lord.

"I lift up my eyes to the mountains, from where will my help come? My help will come from the Lord who made heaven and earth."

When I read your email, I knew I had to share this with you right now.

In Christ,
Scott Chestnut

Okay, if you're reading this book and you don't have goose bumps after that, then you're the fruitcake, not me.

When Sunday rolled around, I went to church. Yeah, you guessed it. We sang a song based on *Psalm 121*. God kept confirming His word to me. He kept telling me that I wasn't nuts and that He really did audibly call me by name and lead me to a Bible verse on a mountain in North Carolina that I had never set foot on in my life until that day. He froze me in midair like some Star Trek tractor-beam just like he froze Mitchell Paige on Guadalcanal.

15

URGENCY

Why did it take me 12 years to start writing this? Good question. This experience left me sort of awestruck—in a wonderful way. But when God gives you something like this, you don't want to treat it with disrespect or be flippant about it. I kept waiting for the Lord to lead me. Maybe this was a miracle just for me and not to share with the world. Maybe it was supposed to be a part of that hidden life just between me and Jesus. Maybe it was as simple and profound as the verse, *"My help comes from the Lord . . ."* Or was it His words to me, "Johnnie, walk a little farther with me." A good man recently told me that after reading this manuscript, he looked up the Hebrew meaning of the word "walk" and it is this: To go on *habitually*.

Don't think I have not worried about it. Am I failing Him? Am I walking farther with Him or just plodding along on my own path again? I just did not know what I was supposed to do. Then one morning at around four o'clock I awoke with an almost urgent need to write this story. Yeah, the word is "urgent," and I have a history with that word.

I try to be aware of the leading of the Holy Spirit in my life. I sure don't handle situations like I should sometimes, but I think God knows I'm trying. There is a real risk of sounding like a fruitcake or a fraud, but I felt led to finally write the story, no matter the risk. I felt an urgency to write it. In my life on more than one occasion I have felt an urgent need to try to lead someone to Christ. Why urgent,? I don't know, but no other word seems to fit.

Eddie Pritt was my best and dearest childhood friend. I wrote about him earlier in this book. I want to give you a very short version of his life. Eddie and I remained best friends even after I moved to Florida. Eddie flew to Florida during the summer, and we trained together for high school football. He had me drinking concoctions of a dozen eggs and bananas and protein. He taught me how to properly train with weights. Eddie could bench press four hundred pounds. He made All State linebacker in Charleston. After graduation, he married his high school sweetheart, Carol. He just adored Carol, and she was nuts about Eddie.

Carol was an heiress and inherited a portion of her inheritance every five years. Eddie told me that that small percentage of the total was enough to live on the rest of their lives. But they were not settling back. They were both very ambitious.

Eddie got a full ride to play linebacker at Virginia Tech but turned it down for a full ride in chemical engineering. He then decided to become a doctor and was a top grad in medical school at West Virginia. He was brilliant. They did not need money, and Eddie's goal was to be a doctor and remain in West Virginia. He told me that too many doctors were leaving for other states where they could make more money. Eddie had a great heart, but I wasn't sure that he was saved, or maybe I just took it for granted because I loved him.

They lived in an apartment in Morgantown, West Virginia, while Eddie did his internship. One night Eddie was working the emergency room in Morgantown when he was alerted that the victim of a bad car crash was coming in. When they wheeled in the victim, he saw that it was the love of his life, Carol. She was dying. A coal truck had crossed the center line and hit her head-on. Eddie could not save her.

He fell apart. He went from a guy who was built like a linebacker and had been a state shot put champion down to 160 pounds. I got him to come to St. Pete for a two-week visit about eight months after Carol's death. He was trying to come out of it, but he was in terrible pain. At night, Nancy and I could hear him through our adjoining bedroom wall having nightmares. This was a new one for me, hearing somebody else having nightmares. One morning he came out of the bedroom and his bottom lip was a bloody mess from nearly biting clean through it.

One day I had a friend over named Jim. He was the brother of the guy who got me to go on the blind date with Nancy. Jim was an intellectual, and I liked him. The three of us had a few beers together and gabbed about a lot of stuff. Somehow during our conversation, Jim started talking to Eddie about God and the Bible. Jim had read yet another book, and it was clear to him that the Bible was all a myth or something to that effect.

Hearing Jim spouting his intellectual foolishness was irritating, but when Eddie began totally agreeing with him, I was stunned. Then I was absolutely shocked to hear Eddie as he began to blaspheme the Lord. I guess I lost it and told Jim to get out of my house before I put my foot up his rear end. He left.

Then I faced my lifelong best friend. I was so angry and disappointed. I didn't know what to do, but I had to hear him say that he didn't really believe that crap he'd just spouted. And I had to hear him accept Christ right then. This was not just my Irish temper or Marine Corps logic. It felt urgent to me. It could not wait: it had to be settled.

Here was this man who'd been my best friend since we were four years old, and it was as if I didn't know him at all. I grabbed him by the arm and led him out back to the cement slab that was my home Do Jang. I told him I was suddenly really scared for him. I also told him he was a liar. I told him I was going to beat the hell out of him right then if he didn't admit that he believed in Jesus Christ.

Eddie started crying like a little kid, not from fear of me. It was more like a dam breaking. He then told me the truth, and pain poured out of him. His agony and anger at God after losing Carol was crippling. Then he said it.

"I believe in Jesus, Johnnie." Then he told me the whole story. Carol had been a born-again Christian. She loved the Lord and had Bible studies in their Morgantown apartment all the time. He said, "I would go into our bedroom and turn up the TV. I refused to have anything to do with God or Bible studies. I don't know why. I just had this arrogant attitude.

"I'm angry! I'm so angry at God for taking Carol away from me! He did it to punish me!"

It was a powerful and tear-filled time together. But when it was over, I did not fear for Eddie's salvation any longer. He confessed Christ to me, and I had a peace and so did he. By the time Eddie flew back to Charleston, things looked a lot better. He seemed to be healing.

Two weeks later, Eddie died in a car crash. Was that moment in my backyard a saving moment? I don't know, but I think so. After the funeral while talking to some of Carol and Eddie's friends from Charleston and Morgantown, we learned that they had been praying for Eddie to accept Christ. They didn't think he was saved.

When I told them this story, they rejoiced in God's answered prayer.

* * * * *

Another day on that same backyard Do Jang after class ended, I began to talk to one of my students. His name was Scott Houtz. He was one of my green belts. Scott was finishing college and working at a 7-Eleven store and engaged to be married. Scott had told me a few weeks earlier that he had been robbed at gunpoint on the night shift at a Tampa store.

Scott wasn't a Christian, and I guess I was trying to witness to him. Yes, as his Tae Kwon Do master, I had a bully pulpit, I suppose. But I was really worried about him. He was a wonderful young man who worked his butt off. He told me that he was now at a new store in St. Pete, and he thought it was a lot safer than the one in Tampa. He said there was nothing to worry about.

Look, I don't know why, but I was suddenly overwhelmed with concern for Scott. I told him I was worried about him, but I wouldn't have to worry about him if he was a Christian. We had a long talk, and I may have shown him some scripture—I don't remember. I may have jokingly told him we were going to free spar until he found Christ. I tend to do stuff like that and, yes, I know it sounds bad on a lot of levels. We laughed, and eventually he opened up about his life and admitted something was missing. Scott accepted Christ at my kitchen table. A short time after that Scott was murdered during another robbery just a block from St. Pete High School.

* * * * *

I trained and taught martial arts for about a year with a big black guy named Ruben Coffey. We became close friends. Ruben had a wife and a little boy. One day Ruben's wife called me and told me that Ruben was in the hospital with some kind of blood problem. No one thought it was serious at that time, but he wouldn't be training for a little while.

I went to see him. He had lost some weight, but he seemed perfectly fine and nearly as strong as ever. He was in great spirits and not concerned at all. I told him to call me when he got out, and we'd start training again.

I went home thinking all was fine. That night as I talked to Nancy about Ruben, I started getting concerned. Once again I felt an overwhelming need to make sure my friend was saved. Why? I have no answer other than the leading of the Holy Spirit. He seemed as big and strong as ever, so why was I suddenly losing sleep over it? There was no indication that there was anything seriously wrong with Ruben.

It kept bugging me for a couple of days, and I finally called up a Christian buddy named Greg Beaton. Greg was one of my instructors, and he knew Ruben too. I told Greg I wanted him to go with me to see Ruben and that I wanted to talk to Ruben about the Lord.

We bought a Bible. When we walked into his room and handed it to him, Ruben seemed shocked. Typically, my conversations with Ruben had been about martial arts or the usual stuff about lives and wives. But this day, Greg and I talked to him about Jesus. It took him a minute to adjust. We probably looked like a couple of Jehovah Witnesses walking in like that. But Ruben knew I was a Christian, and he was open to talking about faith.

Ruben confessed that he had been raised in a Christian home but never gave it much thought after he grew up and had gone his own way—like most of us do. It was a good talk, and we prayed with Ruben. Both Greg and I think he accepted Christ right there on that hospital bed.

About a week later, Ruben Coffey suddenly died. At the funeral, I met his father and discovered that Ruben's dad was a pastor. He told Greg and me that he had been praying for his son to get saved for years. We told him our story, and he was so happy and hopeful that it made us all pretty emotional.

* * * * *

So why did I wake up at a ridiculous hour and start writing about this miracle after twelve years? It's a simple answer and, yet, not so simple. The answer is because it suddenly felt urgent. Now, I hand it over to the Lord and wait and really hope this is His will and that it will serve His purpose.

I have had so much fun! Just thinking about what Jesus Christ did to me and for me on that mountain has given me so much joy every day since it happened. When God lets you experience something like this, you want to grab friends who are not Christians and shake them by the neck. I wanted to shout it from the rooftop that Jesus is real! And He really does know us by name!

I'm not saying that I don't still get depressed or angry or worried about all kinds of crap. Right now, I'm facing a surgery and a little battle with cancer, so let me just say that I'm not a joy to be around all the time. And I'm still no pillar of Christianity. When I see the Bible or Christians or my country attacked, when I see common sense treated with some politically correct insanity, it makes me want to beat the tar out of certain people—I still might if they meet me on the wrong day. I worry that I have not changed one bit, I haven't grown enough as a Christian, or that I'm failing to do something I was supposed to do with this miracle.

But after twelve years, I woke up with this urgency. All I can do is hope that I'm being led to write this book. I have no ulterior motive other than wanting to praise God and tell people that He is as real as you and me. He really does know us by name, and He really does take a personal interest in His kids. You don't have to go to church six days a week and sing in the choir on the seventh. He loves even his dirty kids, and we really are His kids when we've accepted Christ. He forgives us for being scumbags if we are sincere when we ask Him to. All the things we always want to believe about God don't even touch just how wonderful and loving He is to His kids. That is what this miracle means to me.

Of course there is a catch. You got to be one of His kids. Scripture tells us that the Word of God would be nonsense to the natural man, the intellectual man. I've seen this over and over in my life. I've seen little kids read a verse in scripture and understand it, while one of my friends, who considered himself an intellectual, read the same verse and said, "This makes no sense." That intellectual friend was Terry, the guy who got me to go on a blind date. He died at forty years old, and I sadly believe he is in hell for eternity.

If you're not a Christian and you still read this book, there are hundreds of verses that will answer your questions. If you aren't saved but you really want to know if God is real, then *ask Him*! As we used to say in Nam, "There it is, Bro." God made it that simple, and that's why He tells us in *Romans 1* that *"We are without excuse."* Scripture tells us that you know in your heart that there is a God just by observing nature.

There is this one parable that I really like because it reminds me to keep annoying the Lord until He answers me. That's right. Annoy Him like a little kid tugging on His pant leg, a little brat that He still loves who really wants something.

The parable that Jesus told is in Matthew. It's about an old widow who was seeking justice from an ungodly judge. This judge could not have cared less about the widow, but she kept hounding him day after day until even an unjust judge finally gave her justice—just to shut her up.

Then Jesus tells us that if this poor widow finally got justice from this evil judge by asking over and over . . . Duh? Do you think a just and loving God is going to do less for one of His kids? God tells us to be persistent. He wants you to ask and keep on asking. Knock and keep on knocking until He answers. So if you want to know if He is real, ask and keep asking for Him to show Himself to you. He promises that those who seek Him will find Him.

If you feel like you'd be committing intellectual suicide to believe in the God of the Bible, then I challenge you. The Bible is the most documented book on the planet. It has prophesied the future for a couple of thousand years, and it's been one hundred percent accurate. There's a world full of proof besides the scriptures if you really want to find it. Just observe nature. Ask God to show you, and then keep on asking.

As I sit here writing the end of this book, I believe with all my heart that we are in the *End Times*. There's some fascinating prophesies in the Bible, but prophesies about Russia becoming allies with Iran, Syria and Arab peoples has always intrigued me. They will come against Israel. That is in *Ezekiel 38 and 39*. But whether the clock is ticking on this planet or not, we all know that the clock is ticking on each one of us. Nobody is leaving here alive.

Is that my urgency? Or am I running out of personal time to write about this miracle? I don't know. But what can it hurt to investigate the Bible and seek to know if Jesus is real? Find a Bible-teaching church and challenge God to teach you. Get alone and talk to Him and find out for yourself.

I have always signed my books with the verse *John 15:13. "There is no greater love than this; that a man would lay down his life for his friends."*

219

I've seen guys do that in the Marine Corps. I am in awe of such sacrifice and love. But sending my only son to be tortured and nailed to a tree to pay for your sins . . . I don't love anybody that much. Only God can love like that. It is so easy to be saved, and maybe that's why we humans—and various denominations—try to add something to it to make it more difficult.

The penalty for our sins is death and can only be paid for by the sacrificial blood of the Lamb of God, Jesus Christ. His Son paid for our sin just as prophesied. You don't have to suddenly start acting like a preacher or be a missionary in Nigeria. You are not saved by your good works. Good works will happen, but they don't save you. We're never going to be perfect until we get to heaven.

If you have never asked the Lord into your heart, then do it now. Confess with your mouth and believe in your heart that Jesus is Lord. What do you have to lose? You are going to croak either way. If Jesus is who He said He is, then you just won the jackpot of all jackpots. Scripture tells us that God has wonders in store for His kids that are beyond our human imagination.

1 Corinthians 2:9: *"Things which eye has not seen and ear has not heard, And which have not entered the heart of man, All that God has prepared for those who love Him."*

Most of the people who read this are already saved, already Christians. We Christians need to give some thought to the Hebrew meaning of the word *walk: "To go habitually."* Are we making Jesus a habit in our lives? Maybe it's easy for you, or maybe it's difficult, but I think the instruction is clear and simple. We shouldn't do anything without including the Lord. If we talk to Him constantly about everything, then I believe we develop a habit. How can you be a close friend to someone that you don't confide in? And not just laying out all of our complaints or needs or desires, but talking to Him about every blessing or moment of joy. It becomes a habit after a while.

I was told a long time ago that if God says something, it means something, and if He says it more than once, you'd better listen. The Bible uses the word "walk" 212 times. It uses "walked" 122 times. It says "walketh" forty-one times. It says "walking" thirty times.

Here are just a few, but they encourage me, and I hope they encourage you. I love the story of

Enoch. Enoch wasn't a Christian for his first sixty-five years on earth. But then he became such a strong and faithful friend of God that he walked with God for the rest of his long life and walked right into eternity with his best friend.

Genesis 5:22-24

Then Enoch walked with God three hundred years after he became the father of Methuselah, and he had other sons and daughters. So all the days of Enoch were three hundred and sixty-five years. Enoch walked with God; and he was not, for God took him.

Genesis 17:1

Now when Abram was ninety-nine years old, the LORD appeared to Abram and said to him, "I am God Almighty; Walk before Me, and be blameless.

Revelation 3:4

'But you have a few people in Sardis who have not soiled their garments; and they will walk with Me in white, for they are worthy.

Genesis 6:9

These are the records of the generations of Noah. Noah was a righteous man, blameless in his time; Noah walked with God.

Deuteronomy 10:12

"Now, Israel, what does the LORD your God require from you, but to fear the LORD your God, to walk in all His ways and love Him, and to serve the LORD your God with all your heart and with all your soul.

Isaiah 2:3

And many peoples will come and say, "Come, let us go up to the mountain of the LORD, To the house of the God of Jacob; That He may teach us concerning His ways and that we may walk in His paths." For the law will go forth from Zion and the word of the LORD from Jerusalem.

Micah 6:8

He has told you, O man, what is good; And what does the LORD require of you But to do justice, to love kindness, And to walk humbly with your God?

Psalm 23:4

Even though I walk through the valley of the shadow of death, I fear no evil, for You are with me; Your rod and Your staff, they comfort me.

Let's all walk a little farther with Jesus.
Semper Fi,
> Love in Christ,
Johnnie M. Clark

THANKSGIVING DAY
November 22, 2018

Made in the USA
Middletown, DE
23 May 2021